the
other
side
of us

A MEMOIR OF TRAUMA, TRUTH, AND TRANSFORMATION

molly weisgram

THOMAS NOBLE BOOKS

Wilmington, DE

Author Contact: **mollyweisgram.com**

Thomas Noble Books
Wilmington, DE
ISBN 978-1-945586-29-3

First Printing: 2021

This book is not intended to provide medical advice or professional services. It is a personal account of one family's experience with Guillain-Barré Syndrome. If you are concerned that you or someone you know might have Guillain-Barré Syndrome, consult a physician. If legal, psychological, or any other expert assistance is required, please seek the services of a competent professional.

dedication

My beautiful children, I am humbled by your spirits. Awed
by your tremendous love. Proud of your efforts. Honored
to be your mother. I want you to know that all is well,
even when it doesn't seem so. There will be times when
life falls apart. There will be times when life comes together.
Separation and reconnection are the natural flow of life.
At all times, listen to the beautiful silence. It is constant.
It will embrace you, love you, and guide you to what you
deeply desire.

I lay this book at your feet. It wasn't a happy chapter in
our lives, but it proves that what inspires deep thought and
growth and perspective—while not always comfortable
—is a part of Joy.

Love you forever and no matter what.

when

the shoe drops

romance is a matter of perspective

I see you falling

we go together but separate

the long way

Mother Mary, pray for us

teach us how to live

the stuff of dreams

reawakened

on the other side of life

the ultimate destination

home

table of contents

1

when

the shoe drops

romance is a matter of perspective

I see you

falling, we go

together but separate

the long way

Mother Mary, pray for us

teach us how to live

the stuff of dreams

reawakened

on the other side of life

the ultimate destination

home

February 12, 2019

It was a nothing special Tuesday night. I was clomping around the kitchen, still in my heels after work. Ground hamburger for tacos sizzled on the stovetop. Eight-month-old Hannah bounced on my hip to the playlist on Alexa while I stirred the contents of the pan.

"Daddy's home!" I said in a singsong voice when I heard the garage door rumble. The corners of Hannah's mouth curled into a gummy smile, exposing the freshly cut nubbins of her bottom two teeth. Chris entered through the back door with a gush of cold air. Ben, age eight, followed close behind. Samuel, age six, and Isaac, age three, were next. They giggled as they discarded their coats and boots in the mudroom. The boys soon poured into the kitchen, each vying for attention from baby Hannah as they passed. "Wash your hands!" I chirped, but it only added a few moments of calm before they began to circle the kitchen island like vultures, picking off a piece of lettuce here and shredded cheese there. I swatted their hands away.

Not a half hour later, everyone was fed and the boys had scampered to another room. Chris held Hannah while I cleaned the kitchen and prepped the following day's dinner with the remaining hamburger. An oven-ready meal always made for a smoother tomorrow. I combined the ingredients, rolled the meat into balls, and ladled tomato sauce over top. Then I covered the casserole with a clank and pushed it into the refrigerator. I took a deep breath.

I couldn't help feeling guilty as I moved from one task to the other. I wanted more time to connect with my family, but there isn't a lot of extra time or energy for that when you are a working mother with four children under nine. Still, I was irritated with myself. A subtle sense of anxiety had crept into my life, and I couldn't decide if it was a case of postpartum depression, divine discontent, or a call for a beefed up gratitude practice. Whatever it was, I judged it as a blatant disregard for the many blessings in my life. I knew better, but I couldn't help feeling a nagging sense of… something.

I didn't talk about this with Chris, though. He and I crossed paths just long enough to debrief the day's happenings. He had conducted a strategic planning session for a client and had been on his feet both literally and metaphorically all day long. He reported that his event went well, but he wasn't feeling the best. I looked him over. He appeared healthy enough. I asked if he planned to go to the doctor. He said he'd already set up an appointment for the following day. My question was more of a challenge, and I had not expected his response. I nodded, surprised, but silently praised his initiative. I thought nothing more about it as I ushered the children to their baths.

I visited with a friend by phone before I toppled into bed that evening. I told her about my rising anxiety. "I have everything I could ever want," I said. "A wonderful husband, healthy kids, supportive parents, a good job. But instead of colorful, vibrant joy, which is the way I should be feeling, I feel nervous. Like I am waiting for something bad to happen."

"It almost sounds like you are experiencing a feeling of dread."

Dread.

"Actually, yes!" That felt right. Along with anxiety, guilt, and exhaustion… dread. "It's ridiculous, though," I replied.

2

when

the shoe drops

romance is a matter of perspective

I see you

falling, we go

together but separate

the long way

Mother Mary, pray for us

teach us how to live

the stuff of dreams

reawakened

on the other side of life

the ultimate destination

home

February 13, 2019

The next morning, Samuel was sick and unable to go to kindergarten. Rather than the usual scramble to split duties, Chris offered to stay home with him even though he still wasn't feeling well himself. I sensed that he was eager to get to the clinic when I called to touch base. I half-jokingly asked if he wanted me to join him for the appointment. He accepted the offer without hesitation. I wrinkled my forehead. I didn't even know his symptoms. "What are you feeling?" I asked. He described numbness and tingling in his hands and feet. I had a vague recollection of him fiddling with his hands, squeezing one and then the other, but he had self-diagnosed himself with carpal tunnel years before. I immediately assumed this was related. I wasn't too worried, but I agreed to join him.

When we arrived at the doctor's office, we were ushered into an exam room by a nurse whose son is friends with one of ours. We chatted about the weather and our boy's scouting efforts between answering routine health questions. I felt embarrassed to be there with Chris. I had always downplayed health issues, even minimizing my own pregnancies, so my participation in Chris' appointment felt like an unnecessary amplification of the situation. I fully anticipated that he would be sent home with a list of recommended stretches, anyway.

A knock on the door. Dr. Dan Rasmussen, the physical medicine and rehabilitation physician and our longtime friend, entered the room. Not having previously met in this professional setting, we shook hands. Dr. Rasmussen listened to Chris as he described his symptoms and then conducted a physical assessment. He asked Chris to ball his fists and then bump them together in front of his chest, elbows out. Dr. Rasmussen applied downward pressure and instructed Chris to push against it as he lifted his elbows. The physician pushed down, but Chris could only hold one of his elbows up. His right shoulder was considerably weak.

"Huh, that's weird," Chris said with surprise. He had no idea.

Dr. Rasmussen took a step back. "I don't like that. I don't like that at all." He sat on his rolling stool and reiterated the symptoms while trying to match them with possible causes. I watched his eyes search the corners of his mind as he talked. He named a series of unpronounceable diseases, including one called Guillain-Barré Syndrome that he quickly dismissed by saying, "But that's super rare." Chris spent the next several hours getting x-rays, blood draws, and an MRI.

We received the results toward the end of the day. "All clear," Dr. Rasmussen said. A sense of relief.

"That's good, but I still feel like something is off," he continued. "I don't like the weakness in that arm. Because it's nearly five o'clock, I think you should go straight to the emergency room to get a spinal tap. That will help us determine what, if anything, is going on. You might consider staying overnight at the hospital for observation, too. If there would be a problem in the middle of the night, I wouldn't want you to have to worry about the kids."

Chris and I looked at each other. I waited for him to lessen his symptoms if for no other reason than to avoid a spinal tap, but he surprised me again and agreed without hesitation. Before we went to the emergency room, we picked up the children from school and delivered them to my parents' house. "Dad just needs to get a few more tests. No big deal," we said as they crawled out of the car.

When we arrived at the hospital, we checked in at the registration counter and waited to be seen. Chris was his normal cheery self, but he was determined to see this through. *What are*

we doing here? I wondered as I looked around. Chris hadn't
been sick as far as I could tell. In fact, he had played city league
basketball just a few days before. He'd joked about getting old
after making a few clumsy moves on the court, resulting in a
pulled groin and jammed finger. Overall, though, he had been
feeling great. Except for the tingling hands and feet and the one
other symptom he described: an unusual sensation. The previous
day, when he walked into his strategic planning session, the
February wind had plastered his pant leg to his skin. Nothing
unusual about that. Not in South Dakota, anyway. But when the
fabric touched his leg, he said it felt like the area was drenched
with water. This clearly troubled him, but I didn't think it was
the strangest thing I'd ever heard. At any rate, it wasn't alarming.
And it didn't explain why we were in the ER.

In a small exam room, I watched Chris roll into a ball before
the needle entered his spine to extract a sample of fluid. I couldn't
help but think back to my epidurals before childbirth. It was
definitely different watching from this angle. We spoke with the
ER physician after the procedure was completed. Chris didn't get
directly to business. As usual, his conversation first focused on
relationship connections, sports, and hometowns. Only then did
the doctor tell us the results of the spinal tap. Clear fluid, not
cloudy. He said everything pointed to a virus and recommended
some "good old-fashioned rest and chicken noodle soup." We were
ready to put this episode behind us.

We spoke with Dr. Rasmussen by phone as we drove home.
Even after we described the all-clear test results, he asked if Chris
planned to stay at the hospital that evening. We looked at each
other over the car console, brows furrowed. "It doesn't really seem
necessary, does it? All the test results came back clear. The ER doc
recommended chicken noodle soup. It probably makes sense to go
to bed and get some rest," I said.

"Are you sure?" Dr. Rasmussen replied. I turned to Chris.

Chris hedged before saying, "Yeah, I will probably just go home and see how it goes."

We entered my parents' house and greeted the children. I was in search of dinner when I heard Chris say, "Molly, we need to go back." Not my proudest moment, I reacted by laying my head on the kitchen counter. My dad reflexively placed an encouraging hand on my shoulder. After accepting my parents' offer to keep the children overnight, we casually told the children on our way out, "The doctors just want to make sure Daddy is all right. Everything will be fine. Okay? Love you! See you tomorrow!" The door slammed behind us.

"Why did you change your mind?" I asked as we climbed into the car. He explained that when he walked through the house, he couldn't control his legs. He staggered and had nearly fallen. It scared him. We called Dr. Rasmussen to accept his offer to stay overnight at the hospital after all. I could tell by his voice that he was relieved.

The cold winter evening automatically had me walking at a brisk pace to the hospital entrance before I realized Chris wasn't next to me. I looked behind and saw him hunched over and hobbling. His body seemed to be aging by the moment. Horrified, I backtracked and steadied him inside. Chris and I both felt more secure after being tucked into the hospital room. It was warm and reassuring to be settled, surrounded by medical professionals, as Chris continued to decline. His legs felt heavier. He was experiencing discomfort especially in his lower back but after a dose of pain medication seemed relatively unfazed. I allowed myself to rest through the evening hours in the corner chair with a hospital blanket. My mind wandered to the fabric tucked under my chin. The last time I had felt this kind of blanket brush my face was eight months earlier when we'd been in this same hospital, two floors up, comforting our newborn.

February 14, 2019 | morning

Six-thirty in the morning. We straightened ourselves for the physician's visit. I was feeling confident, and the previous day's test results gave me good reason. Chris expressed gratitude that there wasn't a tumor wrapped around his spine. I recalled my unexplainable feeling of anxiety. I had sensed dread, but I didn't know it was Chris' dread. He hadn't given me any indication of fear even though he now confessed that he'd been fear dreaming for a few days before admitting to "not feeling the best."

With a quick knock, the physician on duty entered the room. He conducted a physical assessment in his swift and sure way. I watched him squat down to tap Chris' knees with his little rubber hammer, carefully observing the response. Finally he stood up, nodded, and ran through Chris' symptoms and test results from the previous day. Tingling and numbness in the hands and feet, weakness in the arm, decreased mobility in the legs, clean scans and blood tests. He then explained that after consulting with the neurologists at the tertiary care center in Sioux Falls, they agreed that everything pointed to Guillain-Barré [*gee-YAN-buh-RAY*] Syndrome. The disease that Dr. Rasmussen had described as super rare.

The morning's physical assessment was confirmation. Chris had no reflexes, not even the slightest jerk in response to the tap of the little rubber hammer. It was a tell-tale sign. The physician asked if Chris had had a cold or a stomach bug in the past few weeks. Chris shook his head no. Flu shot? Yes, but it was back in November. No connections there. The physician explained that only one in every 100,000 people in the world get Guillain-Barré Syndrome each year. The cause is unknown, but the disease is often triggered by a simple virus or bacteria. He said Guillain-Barré Syndrome sets off an auto-immune response in the body. Rather than the immune system attacking the virus or bacteria, it attacks itself, specifically the nerves. The first symptoms typically emerge as tingling in the extremities.

This was not the first or even the second time we'd heard of this disease in the last twenty-four hours. Dr. Rasmussen first introduced it as a possibility, but Chris' brother Mike had called the previous evening to tell us that the symptoms sounded suspiciously like those described by one of his employees several years earlier. He reported that Guillain-Barré Syndrome left her without the use of her legs for three months.

The physician gave us a biology lesson. "Our body's nerves are wrapped in a special coating called the *myelin sheath*. Think of an electrical wire that is covered in plastic coating. The electrical wire is the nerve, or axon. The plastic coating is the myelin sheath. The myelin sheath is the pathway the brain uses to send messages to different parts of the body, telling it what to do and when. Messages from the brain don't get transmitted when the myelin sheath is damaged, which is what happens when someone has Guillain-Barré Syndrome. This causes paralysis of the body, starting in the feet and hands and progressing toward the core. In severe cases, breathing is affected, and the patient could require a ventilator. However, the progression of the disease is different for everyone. What we know is that once the damage is done, the body will start to repair itself. Physical therapy is typically part of the recovery too. Everyone is different, though. At this point, we just have to wait and see. The good news is that ninety to ninety-five percent of people with Guillain-Barré get back to their lives. You'll get back. It might just take some time."

He explained that there is a treatment for Guillain-Barré Syndrome called *Intravenous Immunoglobulin Treatment* (IVIG). Chris needed to begin it immediately. The treatment wouldn't cure the disease, but it could stop the progression. And the sooner Chris got it, the more likely it was to be effective. Chris would be airlifted to Avera McKennan Hospital in Sioux Falls to receive this treatment.

In an odd way, I felt like we had hit the jackpot. We caught it early. There was a treatment that was effective when caught early. There was a great chance that we would get back to our normal lives. The physician took his leave, and I sat down on the bed facing Chris. I put both hands on his shoulders, steadied myself, and looked into his eyes. "This is going to be the best thing that ever happened to us," I said.

This statement was consistent with our practice. We had a shared understanding. We weren't strangers to ups and downs, not after the last several years of riding the entrepreneurial roller coaster of Chris' various business ventures. The unpredictable life of an entrepreneur provided good incentive for sifting out what is truly reliable in the world. A few of those things: attitude and perspective. Chris had a habit of asking himself in times of frustration or fear, "How is this for me?" In doing so, he exercised the belief that everything is *for him*, rather than *against him*. His daily practice of turning frustrations into teachers had proven helpful.

This would become an understatement.

3

when

the shoe drops

romance is a matter of perspective

I see you

falling, we go

together but separate

the long way

Mother Mary, pray for us

teach us how to live

the stuff of dreams

reawakened

on the other side of life

the ultimate destination

home

February 14, 2019 | afternoon

Valentine's Day. I had never been a fan. It seemed wrong to commercialize love with nauseatingly sweet candies and generic, well, everything. Our society had created a mass narrative on fictitious love in order to sell crap. It screamed inauthenticity and made me crazy. This, however, was a narrative changing day. Even in distress, the irony was not lost on me. It was Valentine's Day, and love suddenly seemed more precious than ever.

We waited with forced patience in the hospital room, becoming more anxious by the moment when we learned the plane was delayed by a snowstorm. I asked the nurse if I should drive Chris the three hours to Sioux Falls instead. I repeated the words of the physician. The sooner Chris had access to treatment, the more effective it was likely to be. The nurse responded by saying there was no way of knowing how this disease would progress, so to be on the safe side, we should stay near medical care. I accepted this without argument, but I wondered which was worse: waiting for treatment or risking a three hour drive.

There was a seat available for me on the flight, so my parents brought the children to the hospital for a quick visit before Chris and I departed. When they arrived, Chris acted the ever gracious host. He explained his diagnosis and the upcoming treatment with a smile. He talked excitedly about the airplane. He assured the children that everything would be fine. There was nothing to worry about. While I nursed baby Hannah in the corner, I watched Ben, Sam, and Isaac examine Chris with their eyes, searching for evidence of his illness.

By one o'clock in the afternoon we were in the sky. It was a beautiful day above the clouds. The sun shone cheerily through the windows, and the hum of the plane was calming. I held Chris' glasses as he lay on the stretcher directly in front of me. The flight nurse watched over him from across the aisle. The nurse was cast in a hazy silhouette with the bright light streaming through the windows behind him. He looked like an angel. He talked to me about Guillain-Barré Syndrome and described the disease process while giving me a gentle preview of the things we might encounter, such as breathing difficulties and ventilators in severe cases. He suggested we take it one day at a time, though. "No two cases are exactly the same," he reminded me.

We arrived at the hospital's emergency room transitional unit in less than an hour. The intake area was separated by privacy curtains, but I could still hear the steady hustle in every direction. Peeking through the curtains, I saw makeshift desks shoved together in clusters. Piles of papers scattered over their surfaces. Someone wearing scrubs, tennis shoes, and a messy bun perched atop her head stood by a desk with a phone sandwiched between her cheek and shoulder. She was flipping through a chart.

We waited nervously for another hour and a half, hungrily accepting the nurse's presence when he parted the curtains and stepped inside to complete the requisite paperwork. He held a clipboard with Chris' chart open for review. I did my best to read his facial expressions as he silently read its contents. Finally he told us we were on our way to the Neurology Brain and Spine Institute. Our neurologist would meet us there.

I pressed myself against the wall as Chris' hospital bed was rolled into the elevator. The doors closed in slow motion, and I felt the heavy pull of gravity as we ascended. My mind wandered to a recent conversation when Chris had admitted to consistently making the effort to get people's attention when walking by them. It didn't matter if he knew the person or not, he intentionally tried to catch their eye. I laughed when he told me he did it for the sole purpose of smiling at them. "Of course, you do," I'd said with a snort. "Just don't be weird about it." I couldn't help but tease him a little for this perfect demonstration of his relational personality.

I wondered if Chris would try to smile at people today. I could only imagine how he felt. Yesterday, he was a strong and healthy 42-year-old, standing tall over the majority of people with his six foot, two inch stature. Today, he was wearing a hospital gown, looking up at the people around him, as his hospital bed was rolled down a public hallway because his legs had stopped working.

The elevator came to a stop, two dings. The doors opened and someone entered. Sure enough, Chris looked at the bystander until he caught his eye. Then he smiled his big smile. The man responded in kind and then looked away. I let my gaze linger on Chris' face, catching a flicker of hesitation pass over it. I wondered if he was having an identity crisis. After all, our sense of identity is largely connected to the way other people view us. And now we were patients.

We trudged down a long corridor lined with hospital rooms. I tried to walk directly next to Chris, but it was awkward. This formation didn't lend to the flow of hallway traffic. I dropped behind, looking like I felt, unable to keep up. Behind Chris, my lens widened. I saw patients in their linen gowns shuffling down the hallway with therapists by their sides. Other patients were vaguely visible in their beds as I stole quick glances through their open doors as we passed. I noticed that some rooms blared with the sound of television, while others were quiet and dark. Visiting family and friends carried coats and wore tired eyes. Most kept their faces pointed to the ground, looking up only briefly before scooting around us. Even in that quick glance, I could see emotion. Everyone was wrestling reality. It was an intimate thing.

I watched the nurses use their body weight to maneuver Chris' hospital bed through the door and into place. Once the bed was settled and braked, we got acquainted with our surroundings. It was a small room, but it had everything we needed: a bed, chair, television, sink, and adjoining bathroom. Things I couldn't imagine needing were there, too: a vital signs monitor, call light, suction tube, and oxygen mask. I noticed the room's bland and cheerless hue and blamed it on the lighting.

On my search for coffee, I learned that the Brain and Spine Institute was separated into clusters that all looked basically the same, except ours was in a cul-de-sac. The rooms in our neighborhood formed a semi-circle around a central nurses' station. Signs that read "fall risk" were taped to our neighbors' doors. I looked back to see if our room was labeled with the same. No sign. The sounds of moaning came from at least one direction. Uncomfortable, I returned to the room and said, "I don't know what is going on in the other rooms, but people are moaning out there. What other diagnoses are being treated on this floor?"

Chris shrugged. Happy Valentine's Day to us.

February 16, 2019

We had oriented ourselves to the revolving door of professional visits. Nursing staff, dietary staff, physical therapists, occupational therapists, respiratory therapists, custodial staff, and physicians made their regular rounds. As soon as we finished with one, another would enter. We told our story again and again, anxiously hoping that the next person could provide additional insight. But Guillain-Barré Syndrome is rare. There wasn't much more anyone could tell us. While the hospital teemed with people, we were relatively alone. Rare is lonely.

The high points were visits from the neurologist and Chris' daily IVIG treatment. The IVIG treatments were safely delivered by a robot named Tug. Tug moved in a smooth and consistent manner, similar to R2D2 in *Star Wars*. But its pace rivaled that of a turtle in a hurry. While we waited during these first few days in the hospital, Chris would sit on the edge of his hospital bed, trying to relieve the discomfort in his lower back. He propped himself up with both arms, using them to balance his torso like kickstands.

I searched Guillain-Barré Syndrome online. Dr. Google said that on average, people with Guillain-Barré Syndrome experience declining physical function for two to four weeks before the process of recovery begins. The idea of being absent from home and work that long seemed difficult but manageable. We could do anything for a few weeks. We used the idle time to consider how to communicate our unusual predicament to family, friends, co-workers, and clients. Together, we drafted a tone-setting email that I sent on Chris' behalf to his client groups. We needed to set the expectation for how to manage in our absence, even though we weren't sure what to expect ourselves.

To: MaxwellStrategiesClients@gmail.com
Date: February 16, 2019
Subject: Sometimes life throws you a curve ball...

Good evening everyone,

Earlier this week I started having some unexplainable health issues, mainly tingly fingers and toes, achy back, weakness, and fatigue. After x-rays, an MRI, labs, and a spinal tap, I was admitted to Avera St. Mary's for observation. Not twelve hours later, and after additional weakness and lost mobility, the experts at Avera St. Mary's and Avera McKennan diagnosed me with Guillain-Barré Syndrome. This is a rare syndrome where the body's immune system mistakenly attacks its own nerve coating, resulting in the nerves being unable to communicate with the muscles and general senses.

I was airlifted to Avera McKennan in Sioux Falls and then transferred to its Brain and Spine Institute, where they are administering a five day dose of IV Immunoglobulin (IVIG). Without this medication, the syndrome progresses for about two weeks before plateauing and then gradually subsiding. This medication works to stop the natural progression of the syndrome and make it subside before it does additional damage.

Currently on day three of the treatment, I have also begun physical and occupational therapy as it is clear that I have some recovery as my body starts to regrow its nerve coatings. At this current point in time, although we will know more in a few days, I anticipate a two to four week stay in the in-house rehab center here at McKennan in Sioux Falls.

This has been such a great example to me of why we all need to consider what matters most today and every day. For perspective, I was playing city league basketball on Sunday (we won by the way:), and by Wednesday, I could not walk.

I cannot tell you how grateful I am. I am grateful for a good prognosis. I am grateful for the skills and contributions of the many caregivers and supportive family and friends. I am grateful for perspective.

As you can imagine, this will have an impact on my ability to work over the coming weeks. However, with the support of the Maxwell Strategies team, we are putting together a plan for what's next and how to continue to move our work together forward.

I believe everything is *for us*. I look forward to seeing how this is true in this experience. I have already learned a lot.

I will be in touch over the coming days. Thank you so much for your support as I transition back home and get back into full life and work mode.

Chris

February 17, 2019

I stepped out of the hospital with a friend to pick up a few essentials. I had packed nothing but my breast pump, computer, toothbrush, contact case, and glasses. I recognized the exhilarating freedom of normalcy the moment I left the hospital. Although we'd only been there for a few days, things like driving in a car, seeing people smile, and walking through a store felt delightful. I extended normalcy with a shower at my friend's house. The water melted the institutional grime from my body as I savored the sweet scents of the bath products.

When I returned to the hospital, Chris watched me coolly as I displayed the things I'd purchased. His distance sobered me, and my new found energy drained away. He apologetically explained that he was happy that I'd enjoyed the time, but he felt jealous. Stuck. The reality was that his arm strength and core balance were becoming more unpredictable. When he attempted to sit on the edge of the bed, I needed to position myself directly in front of his body for fear that he would fall. He could barely hold onto his phone, much less dial it, and the act of maneuvering silverware to cut food was impossible. He struggled to do the things we take for granted every day, such as adjust his glasses, scratch his face, or blow his nose. He resisted asking for assistance because his needs were constant, but eventually the discomfort proved too great and he had to request help. His lower back radiated with pain that crept down his legs when he sat up in bed, and he described the feeling of a band wrapped tightly around his body. He first noticed the band in his lower legs, but with time, it crept upward. The squeeze of the band correlated with the area he was losing most function.

The staff recommended that Chris sit on a special chair for periods of time throughout the day to prompt blood flow. But how do you move an increasingly deadweight six foot, two inch, 215-pound body from a bed to a chair? The nurse aides showed us how. The special chair, which was the length of a bed when reclined flat, was aligned side-by-side with Chris' hospital bed. Three aides reached over the empty surface of the chair and grabbed the edges of the sheet under Chris' body. Bracing themselves against the reclined chair, the aides counted to "three" and then dragged Chris' limp body from one surface to the other. I supported his head during the transfer so it wouldn't accidently bump against anything on the way. Once in the chair, we propped him with pillows so he wouldn't slump over.

Chris was sinking into paralysis like quicksand. It was quietly terrifying. Three days of standing sleepless on the hard hospital floor, watching my husband deteriorate, became a lifetime. I maintained a brave face in public but needed a safe place where I could crumble. The bathroom near the ICU waiting room served that purpose well. It was warm and scented with something that smelled like grandmotherly perfume. When choosing between the two bathroom stalls, I always picked the one on the left. There, I would sit on the toilet with my head on my knees, making ugly crying faces. It was there that I would relax my tense muscles and hide from my current reality. It was there that I could be alone, just for a minute. Then I'd straighten myself out, examine my face in the mirror, and wash my hands in the sink on the right.

I consistently chose the left toilet stall and the right sink. They were mine. It sounds strange, but it was a thing. So much a thing that when I walked into the bathroom a day or two before Chris' impending departure from Brain and Spine and found my stall occupied, I was thrown. I steered myself to the stall on the right. *The other side*, I thought. Once I finished in the stall, I found that the sink on the right was being used by someone else. I steered myself to the other sink. I looked into the mirror and quietly repeated, *the other side*. I continued to repeat *the other side* like a chant until suddenly it dawned on me. I looked to the heavens and said, "Okay, the other side! I get it!" I practically skipped back to the hospital room.

As I prompted Chris to drink water with the straw I brought to his lips, I said with forced calm, "I got a message in the bathroom." He looked at me skeptically. "Oh yeah…?"

"I know it sounds bizarre, but I think we are on *the other side* of this." I explained what had happened. To me, *the other side* meant that the disease progression was reversing and Chris was about to enter plateau. Plateau was the point right before the nerves would begin regenerating, marking the beginning of the healing process. I just knew we were on *the other side*. Something about it felt right.

He dropped his head to the pillow. After hearing me out, he whispered, "I'll take it."

Still, Chris became less and less mobile, and his pain increased. He grew more fatigued. He lost the ability to urinate on his own and was catheterized. He had difficulty swallowing. He stopped eating and then aspirated water. The water I was adamant that he drink. He coughed and sputtered as much as his weak muscles would allow, trying to clear his lungs. I wiped his brow. Packed him with ice. Held his hand. We sat in tense silence.

February 18, 2019

Chris was not interested in watching television, which was unsettling because Chris loved television if for no other reason than to hear it play in the background. But it made sense after I connected the similarities of his experience to that of laboring during childbirth. I hadn't been particularly interested in watching television while laboring either. I assumed there were so many internal changes occurring in his body that he wanted to stay attuned to them. However, to cut the tension, I tried to interest him in one of the programs that might prove calming or inspirational.

I found Oprah interviewing the spiritual teacher Adyashanti on her *Super Soul Sunday* program. This was the kind of stuff Chris and I loved. The spirituality and divinity that we believe connects us all. Adyashanti was exploring the meaning of grace and how even during the fall, or in situations we would consider difficult, the miracle of grace can show up when and where we least expect it. He suggested that if we surrender to whatever is happening and say yes, rather than fight it, we can access the center of existence.

Tears streamed from Chris' eyes as we listened. I put my head on his chest and then looked into his face. I expected him to be lost, despondent, broken, or even angry. Instead, he wondered aloud, "This is a rebirth. What am I going to do with this?" A lump crept into my throat. This was what I would expect him to say in *real life*, but this wasn't real life, was it? It couldn't be real. We were in an unknown place, going to an unknown destination, playing unfamiliar roles. We were the young and healthy. The conquerors of our own destiny. We were the parents who would tell our children that everything would be okay. Weren't we? If we weren't that, then who? Who were we?

By labeling it a rebirth, Chris claimed that we were those people and so much more. We were the people who would be rebirthed. We were the people who would allow the universe to shape us into what it wanted us to become. We were the people who would choose to trust that this pain and uncertainty were *for us* somehow. And although our valley was difficult, and it became downright gut-wrenching, this way of thinking would be our power play. We would control the situation our own way.

February 19, 2019 | early morning

It was the wee hours of the morning, but sleep was not available so we talked. Chris' voice was little more than a whisper, but in that intimate hour, he said, "Let's write a book together. Let's travel the world together. Let's raise great kids together. Let's have fun together." Holding my breath, I dropped my chin and closed my eyes. *How could he be so hopeful right now?* Tears rolled down my face and seasoned the corners of my mouth.

He looked at me. "Perfection is imperfect."

"What does that mean?"

"It means, where you are is where you are supposed to be."

Unbelievable. A new wave of sobs broke forth. The pressure was crushing me, but his words were leavening. He was transforming our current reality into one of divine possibility.

The prescribed five days of IVIG treatment didn't prove helpful for Chris. On day six, things got worse. During his last eight hours in the Brain and Spine Institute, he told us repeatedly in a strained and agonized voice that he couldn't breathe. The monitor showed that his oxygen level was hovering at eighty percent. He was treated for anxiety. I put lavender oil behind his ears and helped him count his breaths. But he responded very slowly. He could barely keep his head balanced on his neck as if he was incredibly intoxicated.

I was concerned but helpless outside of getting ice packs, whispering my support, repositioning his body, flagging the nurse to relay Chris' words, and pleading to the heavens for someone, anyone, to help. Should I be doing something else to advocate for Chris? I was not a complainer. Did I need to be? With my strong and steady husband fading away, I went from concerned to terrified. I was exhausted but also hyper from fear, frightened of the need for tracheal intubation. Adrenaline filled my body. I would have jumped in front of a train if I thought I had a chance of slowing this disease.

Luckily, I was not alone in the descent to hell. Help had arrived in the form of Chris' mother, Barb, who had joined us for the fall. When Chris could suffer his miserable state no more, his eyes rolled back into his head, and his lips formed an oval. His chin stretched toward the sky, and his cheeks and neck sucked in and out as he gasped for the air that was not available. He looked exactly like a fish out of water. His mom and I got inches from his face and sharply repeated his name over and over again. Barb tenderly gathered his face in her hands and tried to coax him back, talk him through his next breath. While I watched Chris' loving mother touch him gently, I resisted the impulse to slap him. A reaction caused by the adrenaline and helplessness. But nothing we could have done would have helped Chris.

Although we were warned that Guillain-Barré Syndrome could affect breathing, I didn't understand what was happening. The care team covered Chris' face with an oxygen mask and whisked him away. Barb and I were left standing in an empty room. Dust bunnies floated across the floor in reaction to the frenzy. Confused,

I murmured, "Was that an anxiety attack?" No. Chris' lung had collapsed due to the elevated carbon dioxide levels in his blood.

We were escorted to a large but empty waiting room after hastily shoving our personal things into hospital-issued plastic bags. I functioned in a dissociative daze until the delayed shock jolted me. I sat down, my head on my knees, and sobbed frantically through gasps of air. Barb gathered me onto her lap, cradling me like a baby. I stammered, "I don't know who I am without him."

She looked at me sharply and said, "Molly, what are you scared of?"

"That… that… he will die."

"Okay, let's go there. If he dies, then what?"

I didn't know how to respond. Barb was no stranger to heartbreak. She had spent the last months of her husband's life camped out in this same hospital.

"I don't know. I guess I will have to figure out how to take care of the kids alone."

"Okay, then what?" she demanded.

I got the picture. She was saying, don't let the fear of what if take over. There is always a way. Her line of thinking sobered me, and the hyperventilating subsided.

Barb said without wavering her voice, "I choose to trust. I know we are taken care of."

She was right. There wasn't anything else we could do. We just had to play it out and trust. I was grateful. Finally, the physician informed us that Chris was out of surgery and settling into the

Intensive Care Unit (ICU). We were redirected to sit in the ICU waiting room until we could join him there. Barb was updating family members by phone when I saw a familiar face round the corner. A friend both Chris and I had worked with in separate professional capacities but who also happened to be the chief executive officer of Avera Health, the healthcare system of which Avera McKennan Hospital was a part. He was holding copies of the pictures I had emailed him the day before. Smiling faces popped off the pages. Our children. The pictures were meant for the wall of Chris' room in Brain and Spine.

Finding a quiet hallway, I slid to the floor. My friend, the CEO, joined me there. I sputtered through sobs with my head on his shoulder. I was a 39-year-old woman with four very young children, two of them still babies. They needed their dad. They needed us. I missed them terribly and wondered when I'd get to hold them again. I was stung by a pang of guilt. When would Chris get to hold them again? I calmed myself by rolling through other facts of our situation. I carried our health insurance through my employment. My parents lived in our community and could take care of the children without major disruptions to their schedules. But the unknown brought me back to dread. When would we get back to our lives? We had disappeared for a full week already, and things were only getting worse. My fear spiked when I thought of Chris' startup management consulting firm that he had put his heart and soul into building. His clients relied on him. Would he be able to keep them and his paycheck?

Sitting next to me on the floor, my friend offered solid perspective and subtle advice. But mostly, he just listened, which is what I needed. Then my mother-in-law rounded the corner. Looking at my friend, she apologized. "Excuse me, Father." She turned to me and said, "Molly, Chris will be ready for visitors in twenty minutes."

With an upturned corner of his mouth, my friend said,
"Well, that's the first time I've been mistaken for a priest."

I couldn't help it. I laughed. I needed that, too.

4

when

the shoe drops

romance is a matter of perspective

I see you

falling, we go

together but separate

the long way

Mother Mary, pray for us

teach us how to live

the stuff of dreams

reawakened

on the other side of life

the ultimate destination

home

As a nursing momma, I was overdue. My chest throbbed.
I ached for my baby. I had been pumping in the hospital bathroom
for a week, surrounded by things that weren't exactly hygienic.
I needed a better plan. ICU personnel directed me to the Women's
Center. I went on a pilgrimage to pump in peace. Once there,
I fell into the most loving arms. Refuge. I hung like a ragdoll as
I described my situation to the Women's Center director. Even
though this was clearly outside of her job duties, she accepted
me without hesitation. She gathered my pump equipment and
carefully washed each bottle and attachment. I watched her
examine the objects as she washed, making the executive decision
to throw away the worst pieces and replace them from her stash
of new parts. Then she wheeled in a hospital grade breast pump
and offered me its use. I accepted.

Sitting on her couch, exposed, I bared my soul. As the milk
meant for my baby gushed out in bloody strands, I shared the
gruesome details of our week through frantic sobs. The onset,
diagnosis, life flight, and descent into hell. I described the trauma
I had just experienced not an hour before as I'd watched my
husband gasp for air like a fish out of water. She looked at me,
really looked at me, with deep, deep sincerity. She told me that
her husband had been in the ICU only a few months before. She
encouraged me to keep pumping and save the milk for my baby.
Then she gave me the code for the employee lactation room.
A new place to escape.

I forced myself back to the ICU, knowing Chris was ready for
visitors. I was terrified to see him. I feared he would be angry. I felt
as if I had failed him. The fact that he could no longer talk because
of the ventilator tubes didn't help. I had never been so lonely in my
life. As I walked into the ICU, I passed staff rolling out a corpse.

I stiffened, the unreal nature of the experience striking deeper. But, beyond the beeping of machines and the critical patients, there was an unexpected calm in the ICU. The staff seemed capable. Ready for us.

I wondered which curtain my husband, my life, was behind. The front desk attendant pointed the way, and I walked down the long corridor, dodging hurried people wearing scrubs and white coats. I peeked around the curtain and crept to Chris' side. I held my breath as I studied him. His mouth was propped open and tubes spilled out. I touched his arm, and his eyes peeked through heavy lids. The corner of his mouth curled into a smile behind the tubes when he saw me, and I relaxed slightly. He closed his eyes.

Confined to Chris' hospital room for the last several days, I'd had little time to rest before Chris' pain would take over and the desperate work of trying to comfort him began again. Seeing him at peace was a deep relief. I was able to let out the breath I'd been holding in for a week. I soon learned that we had been assigned one of the limited ICU family rooms. These rooms with no doors were provided to ICU families who needed a home base. I was incredibly thankful to have been invited to use the space. There was no way I could leave the hospital. Not now. This was a crisis. The family room provided a place for me to throw some cushions on the floor and drop to the ground. An opportunity I took gratefully as Chris had been too restless and uncomfortable for either of us to sleep the last six days.

Barb and I planned to rotate through twenty-four hour shifts. Chris' brother, Chad, who was on his way from California, would work his way into the rotation too. Chris was one of six children in a close-knit family that could have been the model for a Norman Rockwell painting. His family was grounded in love and positivity and had an open armed approach to everyone. Thanksgiving always included new friends. The blessing of his big family: I knew any one of them would back us up.

Later that evening, Chris' night nurse in the ICU, a very capable and very pregnant woman, took the time to sit with me. I shared our story and introduced her to Chris. The real Chris. The one who didn't spend his time intubated in a hospital bed. She listened as I sorted through the events of the last week and described my fears. She quietly, carefully, and honestly provided information about the ICU and described things you might expect from a patient on a respirator in intensive care. Things about anesthesia, pain medications, and something she referred to as ICU delirium.

I thanked her for her time and compassion. She hesitated as she drew back the curtain to leave. Turning around, she said, "Molly, this isn't just happening to Chris." She handed me an ICU journal. The truth of her statement struck me. I felt pinned down. Totally trapped. My insides wanted out, and my outsides wanted in. I wondered if I was slowly going insane. I snatched the journal provided by the nurse and furiously began to write.

February 19, 2019 | ICU journal

Don't die.

I am so sorry. I have so much guilt. You have fallen, and I couldn't catch you.

Maybe you are undergoing a metamorphosis. A firing in the kiln. What masterpiece will you make of yourself?

We have the best life because we are together. Our kids are so special, and I appreciate your influence on them.

I am so overwhelmed with guilt. It's not fair that you have to be poked and prodded, unable to move or talk. Hurting.

I am sick. My body gets numb yet prickles with fear. I know this is a challenge in faith and trust. It's so hard. I am sorry you are going through this. I am so scared. So scared.

Nothing but forever is sufficient.

I don't know how to pray. I have done it somewhat superficially, but when I need to do it most, I don't know how. I am scared that if I pray for truth, bad news will come. That you will go to your ultimate Truth, and I am not ready to let you go.

This guilt is unbearable, and any negative thought I have ever had of you burns in me. Regret. Regret for not always raising you to the light. I am so sorry. You don't deserve this. I love you so much.

I am so much better with you. You ground me. You see things bigger. You roll with it rather than get mired down in the muck. You are an angel here on Earth. I can't let you leave. We need you.

I feel like I wasn't the advocate I should have been for you. You told us what was happening. You had to gasp for air until it was an emergency. I went along with it. I failed you. Please forgive me.

I am not sure what I should be taking care of. Home, work, business, kids, you? We are partners in all things. I want to protect your interests.

I can crumble as soon as I think I have it together. I am strong, and then I am weak. I am confident, and then I'm fearful. Fear has been one of the worst parts of this. What if we lose you? What if you can't do what you want to do when this is "over"?

I am afraid of losing it all. My husband, the father of my children, my partner, my friend, my security, my foundation.

This has rocked my foundation and made me wonder.

I am troubled on so many levels. I have been ready for communication with God. Now, I feel guilty. Did I make this happen? I am communicating such a primitive prayer now. "Help me. Help Chris," is all I can say. I tell God how scared I am and how much I need support. I want healing. I want the strength to keep walking and get through this.

I start to pitch my tent in the valley of death when I am overtired, which is easy to be in this situation. I was strong and grateful all day, and then, just like that, I lost it. One nerve hit with fear, and I was back on the ground in a puddle. Afraid of money, time, communicating to the broad public. My nerves are fried, and I have started talking sharply to others. My foundation feels weak.

We are at the mercy...

Barb tapped my shoulder. Her turn. I staggered to the family room for sleep. Lying in a ball on the floor, I hid under my coat. The trauma, paired with the fact that I hadn't eaten in several days, made me cold. The expression shivering with fear suddenly made sense. I didn't feel safe, and I couldn't stop shivering.

February 20, 2019 | morning

At three-thirty in the morning, I woke unprompted. My face was salty. I stood and made my way back to Chris. The television was playing in the empty community waiting room. I heard the lonely hum of a vacuum down the hall. Drawing the curtain back with a slow and measured tug, I found Chris sleeping soundly. The pain he felt when not under sedation made it screechingly obvious what this was: the sweet sleep of anesthesia. I sent Barb back to the family room and sat down to examine the dimly lit space. Except for the white noise of the ventilator and far away beeping sounds of the ICU, it was quiet. I moved my chair next to Chris and rested my head on his bed. I picked up my pen and journal again.

February 20, 2019 | ICU journal

Thy grace is my sufficiency. What does this mean? God gives us sufficiency for the day. God is sufficient for the day. God is the peaceful presence I draw from, but I forget all the time while wanting to control my outer surroundings.

I love you, Chris. I see you lying in bed and I am so happy you are peaceful. And I miss you. I feel alone out here. I want to go home with you. I want to get rid of all the stuff attached to you. I want to feel your arms around me. Then I'd know everything is going to be okay. That's what you signify for me. Stability, calm, perspective.

I feel like a dog that's waiting by its owner. Just waiting until you come back. Patiently, frantically. I see the irony here. I need to understand, know, my true owner. My true stability and foundation. It feels so cliché, but I look around and recognize this is real.

Chris is lying in a hospital bed on a ventilator, and I am holding his hand. We are here. In this situation that you think happens to other people. I am distraught and lost. A lost puppy. I need to find my true owner so I can be fed, sustained. Chris' soul feeds me, but I am led astray. The Presence is the life-sustaining food, and I need to eat. If I eat, I can feed Chris.

So, I know the banquet is set out, but where do I find it? This puppy whimpers and cries. Hides under the bed. There is a thunderstorm, and I am shaking. How do I brave getting out from under the bed when the sky shakes? It takes resolve and a change of mindset. Rather than, this is going to hurt me... this is going to help me.

We are not afraid of the things we know help us. Are you afraid of an outstretched hand? Grab the hand of God that is inviting you, even coaxing you, out from under the bed. It will be okay, girl, it says. It is okay. Don't worry. All will be fine. Shhh, it is okay. This will pass. I love you.

Molly, dearest, never fear. You are my child, and I Am. You can hear my whisper in your soul. You just need to listen to it. Listen. I am trying to tell you something. It is power and strength for you. Turn within, and I will tell you.

- Let me be on your team.
- I want to coach your team.
- Relinquish control.
- I will lead you to the right spot.
- It will be good, I promise.
- Your shell is breaking open, and that's why it hurts.
- Hand the reins to me, and I will make this right.
- Fear comes when you don't let me lead, and you get lost in the dark.

I need out of my head and into my heart.

February 20, 2019 | afternoon

My cell phone buzzed with nonstop questions. "How's Chris?" and "What's the update?" I was tempted to respond with short, snarky answers like "Bad" or "If only I could figure that out."

The mere thought of replying to these questions exhausted me, so I ignored them all. I didn't blame people for wanting to know. I appreciated their concern, but how was I supposed to describe what was happening, and happening to us, not just him? Our life was falling apart. I was perpetually on edge, free falling in a blur. Even if I could have conjured the energy to respond about his condition, the circumstances changed constantly. It was impossible to adequately describe the facts and feelings in a text before confronting the next set of issues.

That's why I didn't call home either. I desperately wanted to talk to my children and my parents, but I didn't know what to tell them. I wanted to give them good news. But I did not have good news. And if I let them in on the gruesome facts of the moment, I would invite them into terror. Terror I could barely tolerate in my own body. It felt like tubes of Icy Hot running through me. A burning, numbing fire in my guts that radiated out to my limbs. No. Whatever stories their imaginations were creating were better than the ones I could tell them.

So, I stayed silent for now.

5

when

the shoe drops

romance is a matter of perspective

I see you

falling, we go

together but separate

the long way

Mother Mary, pray for us

teach us how to live

the stuff of dreams

reawakened

on the other side of life

the ultimate destination

home

February 21, 2019 | early morning

I couldn't stay silent for long. I refused to respond to individual texts, and I didn't want to compile an email list or use social media to relay our predicament. But no communication wasn't working either. It was recommended that I provide updates through a website called CaringBridge, a forum specifically designed to share health stories. But I resisted that too because I had a preconceived notion that CaringBridge was a prelude to death. I wasn't ready to put Chris into that forum. Furthermore, I worried that Chris' story would become another form of misery masturbation if I disseminated it, and society didn't need any more of that. But once Chris went to the ICU, it was clear I had to say something. And CaringBridge was the best option.

February 13-21, 2019 | CaringBridge journal

Because so many people want to know how Chris is doing and how they can help, I want to honor that love, support, and respect by sharing. So, here goes.

This has been a very difficult week. Our life took a complete U-turn last Wednesday when Chris had a doctor's appointment after noticing some tingling and numbness in his hands and feet. Although nothing was apparently wrong, except for these sensations and some weakness in his right arm, Dr. Dan Rasmussen took Chris through several tests, all of which came back normal. Nevertheless, he recognized that something wasn't adding up. Thank you, Dr. Rasmussen, for continuing to push the issue and supporting us the way you did. Because of this, we ended up at Avera St. Mary's Hospital for overnight observation. With great care overnight and Dr. Phil Meyer's assessment in the morning, Chris was airlifted to the Avera McKennan Hospital in Sioux Falls to pursue treatment for

Guillain-Barre Syndrome (GBS). If you are lucky enough not to know what this is, as I was only a short week ago, I am thankful.

In its essence, GBS is a rare disorder that occurs randomly, typically in reaction to a common virus. To combat what it perceives as the bad guy, the body mistakenly attacks itself and, more specifically, the nerve coatings, which serve to conduct messages from the brain to the body telling it to walk, move, etc., effectively labeling it an auto-immune disorder. This attack on the nerve coatings results in a slow, progressive paralysis of the body with considerable pain that eventually subsides after an average of two to four weeks. The most threatening part of GBS is the progression into the diaphragm and chest, which could weaken the muscles enough to endanger breathing. There are two treatments that are meant to slow the progression so it putters out before reaching its peak, hopefully shortening the duration.

Chris started the first treatment option, intravenous immunoglobulin (IVIG) therapy, last Thursday. This is a five day treatment that is meant to infuse antibodies into the body to help fight the auto-immune reaction. Unfortunately, on day six, his diaphragm was weakened to the point where it could no longer function, causing Chris' lung to collapse. We were whisked to the ICU from the Brain and Spine unit. Chris is currently on a ventilator, which is a happy relief after having the unpleasant experience of being a fish out of water. He is stable, and his pain at times can be managed by sedatives and medication.

Recognizing that IVIG was not as effective as we would have liked, we plan to begin a new treatment called plasmapheresis. This flushes the body of antibodies and resets the blood. We pray this will reverse the progression, bring him to the plateau of this illness, and that he will start regaining strength soon.

The good news is there is a good prognosis. The bad news is this is a game in patience. Chris will regain strength, but we have to patiently wait without the answer of when. They say patience is a virtue, and this has been an excellent lesson in patience and a great reminder that we are not in control. Once Chris' strength and mobility return, he will have a stint with in-patient rehabilitation, where he will retrain his body to move. The current best estimate for in-patient rehabilitation is roughly four to six weeks. There will be continued outpatient therapy back home. We are so thankful that there are places tailored to his needs.

This has not been fun. I promise you. It has reminded me that we are not in control, even if you are a control freak like me. It has challenged me to trust the process. It has also amped my appreciation for all that I have, which is a lot. I am thankful for Chris' mom, Barb, who is here by Chris' side and mine. Barb is a rock, firmly planted in the love of God. I am thankful for my mom and dad who have taken our beautiful children into their loving arms. I am thankful for our family and friends who have stepped up to show how much they care in so many different ways.

Mostly, I am thankful for Chris. He is a big presence. His mind is in the right place. His heart is in the right place. He is strategic and thoughtful and willing. He is solid. He is the absolute best partner and father. I am the luckiest.

Chris regularly promotes the idea that we must focus on what matters most today. So, today, what matters most is showing our love for Chris, knowing (in that deep place of Truth) that all is well, and trusting the process. I keep likening this situation to being fired in a kiln. He is (we are) being fired in the kiln, and what comes out will be more beautiful than we can imagine.

We are accepting prayers for trust, strength (physical, mental, and emotional), and endurance. Thank you. More updates to come.

February 21, 2019 | later in the morning

We have been praying for you all. My heart goes out to you.

Prayers for the family and Chris. As the journey continues, God is good and will continue to heal Chris.

Thank you for sharing. Chris is lucky to be surrounded by a strong and loving family.

These were among the hundreds of comments I received in the first twenty-four hours after my initial CaringBridge post. They came from past and present co-workers, high school and college friends, relatives, neighbors, the children's principal and teachers… even people I didn't know but assumed were Maxwell family contacts. I hadn't expected it, but individually and together, they made me feel loved at a time when I also felt so alone and backed into a corner. Journaling helped me deal privately. Sharing our situation publicly allowed me to be vulnerable while maintaining control at the same time. My decision to use CaringBridge allowed people to love me without me feeling like a victim.

I had trained myself over a lifetime to reject poor-me thinking and a victim mentality. I had learned from my past experiences that when I looked at my situation as something or someone else having all the control, I unwittingly gave away my power. That way of thinking hadn't made me stronger, so I made a practice of rejecting it. My long engrained pattern of avoiding the victim role held true even in this situation. But it also left me without words. I didn't know how to communicate without seeming the victim somehow. So, I held everything inside for as long as I could. When I finally found the way to communicate, my CaringBridge journal allowed me to set the narrative with clear, measured, and honest words. To frame our situation in power and light and hope. To feel nothing like a victim.

CaringBridge was also a way to communicate with my parents. If I felt burdened by the seemingly harmless texts I received, then they were being crushed. My parents, who lived in our small community where everyone knew each other, were inundated with questions. Questions from caring people but questions they couldn't answer. Literally overnight, they had assumed the full-time responsibility for our four young children. They needed to be able to counsel them with accurate information. To complicate matters, because she had been working for Chris part-time in her retirement, my mom had not only assumed parenting duties but had also inadvertently shouldered the leadership of his small company. My journal was a relief for my parents and for me as we faced the many uncertainties.

February 21, 2019 | morning still

Physician rounds were the highlight of our day in the ICU. Each morning, an interdisciplinary team started at one end of the hall and worked its way to the other, stopping in front of each patient's curtain in turn. The lead physician stood in the middle of ten medical professionals and broke down the case, reviewed updated lab reports, and belted out questions that team members were expected to answer in staccato. Our first visit from the team was intimidating. I stood outside the circle, straining to hear what they were saying. Eventually, I felt empowered to step inside the circle and take my place directly next to the physician. They were talking about my husband after all. I wanted to hear every single thing they were saying. Chris deserved real advocacy, and I was determined to understand because when the time came for me to make a decision, I wanted it to be an educated one.

Chris started a six day course of *plasmapheresis* the day after he arrived at the ICU. Rather than infusing antibodies like the IVIG treatment, plasmapheresis removed and cleaned the antibodies from the blood and returned them to his body. This was in an effort to disrupt the confused part of the immune system so that maybe, just maybe, it would stop the progression of the disease. The plasmapheresis machine growled to a start with a heavy rumble, followed by a repetitive noise that sounded like a squeaky bicycle wheel spinning round and round. I watched as the red blood was pulled through the transparent tubes attached to Chris' veins. Yellow plasma dripped into a hanging bag as the blood spun through the machine.

Chris was totally aware, completely paralyzed, and fully in pain at this point in his disease progression. Though he couldn't verbalize it due to the ventilator tubes filling his mouth, his pain was obvious from the agonized expression on his face. It was awful to watch and even more excruciating to know that he had no way to communicate beyond a head nod for *yes* and a shake for *no*. Barb, Chad, the nurses, and I peppered him with questions to determine how best to lend our support. It took multiple questions to deduce the simplest request. And our questions came so quickly that when he finally answered with a head shake, we didn't know which question he was answering. Chris' frustration was clear. We needed a better communication method, *stat*.

Capitalizing on his available mobility, which consisted of little more than a head swivel, the speech therapist suggested a laser pointer taped to his glasses paired with an alphabet board. Chris could spell out his thoughts. We eagerly affixed a laser pointer to an arm of his glasses with tape. The light shot forward, and Chris tried it out by nodding his head up and down, then left to right. The red dot followed suit. I held up a laminated piece of paper displaying the letters of the alphabet, and he spelled out his first words: *Thank you*. He dropped his head back to his pillow, closed his eyes, and took a deep breath. Relief.

Everyone was relieved to have a more sophisticated method of communication, but it was not without its challenges. Chris selected each letter by briefly resting his laser light on the intended letter square. As he made his selections, I tried to keep pace with his surprisingly quick cadence, often missing critical pieces of the message and forcing us to start over. In time, I learned to record the selected letters on a dry erase board as he chose them, rather than hold them in my memory. Sometimes I could finish his sentences for him, but other times I had to decipher the words from the long string of letters. It didn't help that the crudely taped laser light constantly slipped, changing his range of motion. I held the letter board higher into the air on tippy toes to accommodate. My extended arm, neck, and back sizzled with discomfort after holding the board overhead for a lengthy period.

It was worth the pain. Our laser and letter board communication provided a glimpse into Chris' reality. We learned that in addition to his unbearable pain he was experiencing extreme temperature fluctuations. One minute he was steaming hot, so we packed his body with ice. The next minute he was freezing, so we pulled away the ice bags and layered his lifeless body with warm blankets. The physicians weren't surprised by these fluctuations. They explained that Guillain-Barré Syndrome had tampered with Chris' autonomic system. His internal temperature gauge was broken.

Sometimes Chris' messages were long, thoughtful, and complete. Sometimes he would drift to sleep in the middle of writing, leaving a hanging thought. Still, other times, likely due to the strong pain medications and anesthesia, his messages made little sense, almost as if they were part of a dream. It wasn't unusual for both the sender and receiver of these messages to end the laser pointing sessions fully frustrated. For instance, after a translating session, we might end up with the word *neckerchief.*

Looking at him quizzically for an indication of whether that's what he actually meant, he would return the gaze with an exasperated look that seemed to say, "Yes, *neckerchief.*" Our boys had just started scouts in real life, so I had to assume their scouting scarves, called neckerchiefs, had been woven into this particular dream. No matter the rationale, it was obvious that we weren't always sharing the same reality.

February 21, 2019 | ICU journal

I feel like I am doing everything wrong. We work together to spell out the things Chris needs, but it's frustrating. Although we try so hard, it is nearly always wrong. We want so badly to take the burden off of him somehow, but we only give a disappointing lift. I cannot imagine the frustration he is feeling.

He gave me the dirtiest look today, and it felt like many following that. My only guess was that he didn't feel I was advocating well enough for him. Rational or not, I don't know if he even likes me right now. Through the letter board, he asked each of his brothers to hold his hand today. He gave them a sweet, reassuring squeeze. I just got the "I hate you" look. This is hard.

I am sure he has so many feelings. I can't imagine everything he is thinking. On top of that, he is pumped so full of drugs. Who knows if he will even remember this? I hope not.

I miss him. I want to talk to him. Be just us. I want to go have fun. I want family movie night. I want to crawl into the bunk beds and read with the kids. I am so sad.

Yesterday was awful. I got up at two-thirty in the morning to sit at his bedside. I sustained throughout the day. He was so unsettled and in pain. It was horrible to see him like that. I tried to be his voice, and while doing so, I inadvertently injected panic into mine. I was tired and working so hard to help with very little success. A hot mess, I was crying frantically in the waiting room, completely brought to my knees.

All the while I am having a conversation with God. I am bringing my needs and desires. I forget every once in a while and then I bring them back. God, I want this to end. I am sick and discouraged. I want Chris' pain to go away and his strength to come back. I want the ventilator out. I want to go home. I want to see the kids. I want peace and calm. I want to find the okay, even good or great, in this. I am thankful for the communication method of the laser light and letter board, and I hope we can get better at using it or not need it at all soon. I want good news. I want to have the best relationship with Chris. A well-used and bright life.

I appreciate our families. The whole village is swarming around us.

February 21, 2019 | still

I trudged out of the ICU down the long corridor back to the family room and passed Chad on his way to swap places with me. Chad has a special energy. He is a survivor, someone who can buoy those around him, especially in trying situations. I gave him a forced smile and returned to my downcast walk. Behind me, he randomly called out, "He's going to be Governor someday."

"And I'll be the fucking First Lady."

Did I say that out loud? My response echoed down the hallway. I heard Chad laugh, surprised. I was surprised too, but I couldn't help the quirky smile that spread over my face. It was official. I was losing it.

Nothing about this situation was easy. The physical, mental, and emotional pain was unbearable. The only thing that made it tolerable was the support we had from our families. We weren't alone. Barb was there. Chris' siblings took turns. Our children were safely with my parents. I didn't know how I could have carried the burden without them. Silently screaming *mercy*, I strained my eyes for any indication that the nerve damage had ceased and we were headed for recovery. I brought my nose so close to Chris' hand that it brushed his skin as I searched for a millimeter of movement in his fingers.

February 22, 2019 | ICU journal

Hold me today, I am not strong. I feel like a zombie. Not myself. Lost. I want to cheerlead and encourage, yet I feel like a failure, over and over. It is clear that I am not in control, obviously and completely, not in control. So, hold me, guide me, and help me be a willing participant so I can be a witness to all the beauty here. Help me celebrate the wins, even just recognize them.

I keep trying to attack this thing mentally, get a handle on it. I think maybe we are in plateau because things seemed sort of the same as yesterday. Who really knows, though? I can't know. Time is our friend, yet right now it feels like there is no time.

It's the perpetual moment.

It's ironic that I have wanted to be in the moment lately. This experience is definitely forcing me there. But this isn't the moment I want to be in. This is a really hellish moment. Have I done something? Thought something to create this? I know this will make a better, stronger, bigger us. But it feels like hell.

God, give Chris strength. God, give Chris patience. God, give Chris the perfect knowledge that he is whole. God, help me not take Chris' frustration personally. It's a very ego-centric thing to do, but I have gone there. Take that away, wipe it away. Replace it with the knowing that all is perfect and well.

God, be with my littles as they try to sort this out. Ben is being a brave, strong soldier. Sammy is taking his mind off of it all, but when he sees me on FaceTime, he crumbles and hides. He wouldn't talk to me yesterday and instead crawled behind a chair. I told my mom and dad to explain that it's okay to be sad, and any kid would feel that way if they couldn't be with their mom and dad. Isaac just needs a hug. He needs reassurance that he is surrounded by love, love, love. Wish I could be there to give that to him.

Hannah just smiles. She is wearing Chris' smile while he can't.

Just wait and see, this is going to be good. (It has to be... doesn't it?)

February 23, 2019

It was an unusually peaceful day in the ICU. Chris requested television and his glasses, and I breathed just a little easier. He looked skeletal, not having eaten for a week and a half, but when he asked me about the children, I felt like I had my partner back for a few sweet moments. Then he asked me to read him the CaringBridge post and comments. He denied feeling "low" but admitted to feeling "sad." I thought back to what I had read about the disease and said, "At least the progression only lasts two to four weeks. It's been two weeks already. We might be at the tail end of this."

With Chris and his brothers watching basketball, we were attempting to replicate a normal Saturday afternoon when a neurologist knocked on the door. He immediately began to describe Guillain-Barré Syndrome as if it was the first time we had ever heard of the disease. I cocked my head and nodded knowingly. Then he dropped the bomb. Chris was experiencing a severe case of Guillain-Barré Syndrome in which his axon, or nerve core, was affected *in addition to* the myelin sheath, or nerve coating. This would require a longer healing period. Chris could be in his current state of paralysis for a few weeks, months, or maybe longer.

Until this point, our energy had been spent on searching for the sign that signaled recovery. We had been clinging precariously to the hope that recovery was imminent. Hope that had been taken away in a few words. Chris was angry. He wanted to yell, so he spelled out choice words with the help of his brothers. I got quiet as Chris and his family members got argumentative. The icy hot feeling returned to my insides, and I felt disconnected. Like I was watching the scene unfold as an audience member. The physician asked if he could speak with me alone. I nodded and followed him out of the room.

We sat at the nurse's station in the hall. From my angle, I could see through a window into Chris' room. Inside, his family gathered around him, outrage and confusion on their faces. Outside, I visited with the doctor in a flat, professional voice. I told him I was having a hard time absorbing what he'd shared and asked him to repeat it. He broke the disease process into three phases for me: the onset of symptoms, the persistence of symptoms, and the recovery from symptoms. He explained that once the progression of symptoms plateau, there is no way of knowing how long it will take for the muscles to start reactivating.

I wrote each thing he said into the notes section of my phone. I needed to minimize these words, see them for what they were rather than how they felt. I repeated what I had heard and then asked for clarification. The voice coming from my mouth sounded contained. "I understand that this is a very severe case with the axon damage and everything, but I am not clear. Do the nerves still regrow with this kind of damage?"

"Oh yes," he replied. My shoulders relaxed slightly.

"It's just going to take longer than it would have otherwise. The longer his paralysis persists, the more risk he has for complications such as pneumonia or skin issues. The more complications he encounters, the longer his recovery. And, the longer his recovery, the greater chance he won't make a full recovery. But who knows..." My shoulders tensed again.

"People like Chris, who were real go-getters before, have a very hard time. It can make them go crazy."

"Mentally insane?" I braced myself.

"No, it's just really difficult for young, active people."

"I can't believe you have to tell people this kind of stuff for your job. It must be hard." He considered it. I explained that we have four small children and that we don't live in town. That Chris owns a small business. I admitted to not knowing what to do.

With a shake of his head, he said, "That's terrible." I agreed.

As he prepared to leave, I remembered a different physician telling me that if Chris was still intubated after two weeks, he would need a tracheostomy. This would remove the ventilator tubes from his mouth and make a hole through the front of his neck and into the windpipe where a tube would be placed for ventilator access. "If this is going to take longer than originally expected, why wouldn't we do the tracheostomy early?" I asked.

"Remember the part in the movie *Dumb and Dumber* when Lloyd exclaims, 'So you're saying there's a chance!'?" he asked. I nodded.

"This isn't a perfect science. There's always a chance."

I returned to the room and made my way over to Chris. While I had a strange ringing in my ears, I didn't feel completely destroyed. He looked at me for an explanation of what had just happened. I described my conversation with the physician and reiterated the three phases of the disease process. I confirmed that the only thing that had actually changed was our timeframe. There was still a recovery. Chris requested the letter board with a jerk of his head. Next to the expletives written only minutes before, he spelled out, "Let's do this." He looked at me challengingly.

"Yes," I replied. "That's exactly what I was thinking." I meant it.

February 23, 2019 | ICU journal

After a pretty good day today, we took a dive. Bad news from a physician created a tailspin, and the family reacted. Chris was angry and in shock. I felt so sad for him. He spoke to us with the letter board for a while, and then he almost went unresponsive. It's like he could hear what we were saying but was having a hard time communicating. I think his body just wanted him to sleep, but he was feeling hyper aware. As the day went on, communication with him got more and more difficult. We would often lose him in the middle of a word and the message would come back unrecognizable.

I pray, pray, pray he won't remember this part.

So far today seems to be a better day. Pain is relatively managed. Chris has been mentally clear, although, there are blips.

I showed him pictures of the kids. It was so hard. He became overwhelmed and said, "It hurts my heart so much to see the kids." He asked everyone to step out of his room while he felt all that feeling. Later, Chad rephrased and said, "It warms your heart to see the kids." Chris agreed.

Later Chris actually watched basketball. He asked about doing a client update. He asked about the kids. I read him teachers' notes and the CaringBridge site, as he didn't seem to remember me doing it the day before. We even saw a tiny finger wiggle. We had a fun conversation with siblings. Then we had a great couple's moment. It felt like I had Chris back. He was there, and it was just us.

At midnight, he called Barb, Chad, and I back from the family room because he needed us. Unfortunately, we couldn't quite understand what he needed other than our company. He obviously wasn't tired, but the rest of us were exhausted. Our arms were hurting from holding the letter board almost to the ceiling so he could navigate it. We weren't quite understanding his messages. We needed to sleep. This is frustrating. I am so frustrated. We had a good day, and I still feel frustrated.

Our baby girl is nine months old today. I am so sad we can't be with our kids.

February 25, 2019 | ICU journal

This cloud of sadness is with me as I wake. I am running out
of steam. My throat kind of hurts. My body kind of hurts.
My heart really hurts.

I miss the kids every, every second. It's a dull reality that I keep
pushing back. Everything inside of me wants to be with them
right now. I want to hold them, check in, and tell them we will
never leave them again. But, here we are.

Chris was supportive today. I told him I was sad. He accepted
it without judgment. Later he criticized me, saying, "You are
so frantic. Take a breath." If he had said it with his voice rather
than through a letter board, I would have bitten him back,
but it was true. Then he said, "Maybe you should go to bed."
That was also true.

Later as the respiratory therapist suctioned out the gunk in his
lungs through his ventilator, he experienced a frighteningly low
heartbeat and high blood pressure. The machines screamed
with loud beeping sounds.

He talked of "crazy, vivid, focused dreams."

February 26, 2019 | ICU journal

Today was a good day. It wasn't completely and utterly exhausting,
anyway. Chris didn't sleep a lot, but he seemed rested. Chad
returned to California, but I am so grateful that he was able
to spend the last week with us. He provided real relief. I don't
know how people do this on their own. It has taken a village.

I am thinking about the kids' initiation into all of this. I feel so
excruciatingly awful that I am not with them and them with me.

I want to gauge their emotional wellbeing, hug their beautiful little bodies. I could write volumes on this, but it just makes my heart ache, which isn't productive.

I want to go home tomorrow to be with them and bring them back this weekend, but how do I leave Chris? Things are still in the acute phase. The risk of me leaving and not able to support Chris is probably greater than the consequences of me not seeing the kids, so that's probably what I need to consider. If I can't see them this weekend, though, it may be closer to three and a half weeks before I do. That is too long to be separated. I feel bad that it's longer for Chris. Such a hard situation.

That said, while I feel the difficulty of it all, I feel so grateful that we can look forward to a good prognosis and create a better than imagined, new normal.

We will do this better. Someday. Do this all better.

6

when

the shoe drops

romance is a matter of perspective

I see you

falling, we go

together but separate

the long way

Mother Mary, pray for us

teach us how to live

the stuff of dreams

reawakened

on the other side of life

the ultimate destination

home

March 1, 2019

Living in South Dakota has its benefits. In addition to the beautiful sky, it's easy to know people. Not only did I cry on the shoulder of the hospital system's CEO the day Chris was admitted to the ICU, but the nurse manager of that unit turned out to be a friend. The wife of a teammate from Chris' college basketball days. She had attended our wedding. Even on her days off, she would drop by to check on Chris and find ways to make him more comfortable. Furthermore, our case manager had dated one of Chris' brothers in a past life and was well acquainted with our family. We had spent time together, and I trusted her. While it was strange to be playing these new roles with people from our past, it was an incredible relief. Their professional acuity was impressive but so was their capacity to care.

I love South Dakota.

As we tirelessly tended to Chris in the ICU, people left food, blankets, gift cards, coffee, dry shampoo, and care packages of all kinds in our family room. People were caring for us when we couldn't do it for ourselves, and their demonstrations of kindness left me speechless. I didn't really want anything except for Chris to get better, but the gifts nourished our bodies and comforted our souls.

February 22-28, 2019 | CaringBridge journal

I am sitting here shaking my head in disbelief. Maybe the feeling is better described as awe. The display of love that we have been witness to is overwhelming. With no expectation for any of this, we have received so much. Nearly every need met before we could even say the word. I don't know what to say except thank you.

This week has been a whirlwind. I have learned that life in the ICU is not dull. In fact, it's often a melodrama filled with minute to minute highs and lows. Chris' mom, Barb, and his brother, Chad, and I were with Chris nearly around the clock. We have been working with clumsy success to find an acceptable balance of pain management with a reasonable amount of sedation. All while trying to help Chris maintain his sense of day and night. From my perspective, although paralysis and the inability to verbalize his needs due to intubation are extremely difficult, the pain Chris has been experiencing is the worst.

Chris is dealing with multiple layers of pain. Pain from lying in bed without the ability to adjust himself for comfort. Pain related to wear and tear from past sports injuries. Pain from the GBS-related weakening of his muscles, which inhibits them from holding the skeletal structure together as usual. And nerve pain related to GBS generally. It's hard to watch your loved one in that much pain, but my guess is that it's worse to actually *be* the one in that much pain.

The bright point of the week was our ability to establish a mode of communication that has allowed us to understand how we can help Chris find comfort and also have heart to heart conversations with him, for which I am grateful. With a laser pointer taped to his glasses, he is able to point to an alphabet board and share his thoughts. It is an absolute godsend, and without this ability to communicate, this already very difficult situation would be so much worse. With this method of describing his thoughts and experiences, Chris is able to participate in his care and advocate for his needs.

This syndrome is obviously not affecting his mind. Another point of sweet light.

As mentioned in my previous post, the progress of this syndrome is something to measure week by week rather than day by day. I would say that although there have been a few bumps in the road, it's possible that Chris is in the plateau of this illness. We have seen some flickers of movement in his fingertips and a change in the type of pain sensations he has been experiencing. The new pain sensations can be likened to how it feels when your leg falls asleep and then starts waking up. Although uncomfortable, it has been (dare I say) exciting at times to cautiously believe this to be a natural part of the nerve regeneration process. Chris himself has described these feelings as ones that "hurt but feel great." These tinges of pain serve as a reminder that the paralysis is only temporary.

This is only temporary. Another point of beautiful, bright light.

A dear friend and mentor of ours once asked us this question. "When walking through the valley of the shadow of death, what do you do?" After we looked at her blankly, she shared her recommendation. "Don't pitch a tent. Just keep walking." We haven't forgotten that.

Chris has had exceptional care, and we are thankful for the training, expertise, and heart of each person who has been part of it. I continue to marvel at the devotion of our families, both of which have rearranged their lives to participate in this chapter of ours. And for all of you who have kept us in your thoughts and prayers, shared food and other comforts, and found ways to help carry our load, thank you. Chris said it best when he pointed to the following letters, "Words are not enough to express how grateful we are for your support."

In addition to keeping those who care about us informed, I found writing on CaringBridge to be cathartic. It helped me process my feelings. It allowed me to step back and observe the situation. The little changes amidst the trauma were confusing and dramatic. In contrast, writing a CaringBridge post every few weeks helped me examine the situation from the long view and identify the trend line. The trend line felt trustworthy compared to the momentary drama. I read my posts over and over again, trying to examine them from an outsider's eye. I was under the microscope. What were others seeing? The comments I received continued to lift me up.

What a beautiful testament to love, endurance, and grace under pressure, Molly. Thanks for sharing this. I will continue to send positive energy your way.

Thank you for sharing your struggles. A load is lightened if more people help carry it. We are praying for you and Chris and the whole family. I think of you many times during the day and wish we were home to help out. Take care of yourself, Molly, so you don't get sick. Chris will need you as he improves. Life sure can trip us up sometimes. Love you.

Call it serendipity, or a godwink, or whatever you want... but one of my daily flip calendars for February 21 had this to say and a good thought to hold on to: "Fire is the test of gold; adversity is the test of strong men. Yet O Lord, You are my Father, I am the clay, You are the potter; I am the work of Your hands; Help me see the creativity of Your handiwork in those around me." Indeed, it takes a family and a village to get us through tough times. We are "in it to win," to use a familiar sports metaphor. P.S. I fully expect to see Chris giving a Ted Talk presentation someday about what happens when life throws you that proverbial curve ball!

Chris and family, my thoughts and prayers are with you in this difficult moment. Like in basketball, seldom do seasons pass without a defeat—but we each emerge from the adversity a better and stronger person. That will be you, Chris. Stay strong.

Molly, we are praying for you, for Chris, and for your children and their caregivers. You wrote so beautifully about your faith in God's plan, your love for Chris, and your hopes for the future. It hurts me that the sweet girl I learned to love years ago and her family have to go through this difficult time, but God is with you, and He promises that "all things work together for good to those that love God." Please call or ask your mom to call if there is anything we can do to help.

Molly and Chris, know that the second graders in Ben's class are stormin' heaven constantly for Chris' quick healing and strength for you, Molly, and the whole family! The Kids of Christ say they are going to "tug on Jesus' cloak until he hears us and heals Ben's dad fast!" So sweet! They continue to sing their Divine Mercy Chaplets also, as you know. The children also continue to rally around Ben with constant love and support (still competing for a chair on each side of him at lunch!). May God bless you with healing, peace, and strength during this difficult time!

March 1, 2019 | continued

Both Chris and I ached for our children. It was a topic we hardly broached because it hurt too much. I wanted to save them from seeing their dad in his current state, but considering the severity of his case, it was inevitable. There was no reason to delay any longer. I thought about the conversations we would have as they looked to me for answers. Mothers have a powerful effect. I wanted to set a positive tone without minimizing the truth to help them cope.

Our social worker connected me to the hospital's Child Life specialists. The Child Life specialists helped me anticipate the children's questions and consider their age appropriate understanding. They said every child handles these types of situations differently, but information can ease tension and give a sense of control. We devised a plan. Upon their arrival, we would take the children on a tour of the hospital. Then we would show them pictures of someone intubated and describe how a ventilator works. Finally, we would bring them to the ICU to see Chris. If they were frightened, I wouldn't force them inside. I would give them the choice to see him. The Child Life specialists would be ready to counsel the children after they saw Chris for the first time, just in case it was difficult.

I felt torn. I wanted to talk to my children in their own environment before bringing them to the hospital, but I worried that something would happen to Chris while I was gone. I wouldn't be able to forgive myself if I wasn't there. But when a sudden opportunity became available to ride the three hours home with a friend, I had a choice to make. I shared my fears with Chris. Without hesitation, he recommended that I go. On the letter board, he wrote, "Come back with the kids and your parents tomorrow. Don't worry about gauging them. Don't overanalyze it. Just love them and tell them how much Dad loves, misses, and needs them right now."

March 2, 2019

I sat in the living room of my parents' home waiting for the children to return from school. The sun was setting and the light dim. It felt quiet, warm, and safe. I looked around. Everything felt familiar but different. I let my eyes wander over, *savor*, the evidence of family. Shoes kicked into a corner. School papers piled precariously on the edge of the table. A half-eaten cookie left on the counter. I walked into the bathroom to examine myself in the mirror. I looked different too. I was probably twenty pounds lighter, but there was something else. I looked... broken. My face shattered into a contorted sob, but I swallowed it back. Crying didn't help. I had to be ready for any possible reaction from the children. I expected subtle punishment for having disappeared without warning. I felt I deserved it.

When they arrived home, Ben and Sam walked past me like my presence was not out of the ordinary. "Hi, Mom. What are you doing here?" They kept their faces pointed in the direction of the iPad. I reached for them. My fingers brushed their coats as they passed. Slightly confused, I let out an awkward giggle. Maybe people were right. Maybe children really are that resilient. Three-year-old Isaac walked through the door next. I crouched to his level. He ran for me and jumped. His force rolled me onto my back. I held him tightly, letting go of all else. Then my dad, who was holding Hannah, appeared around the corner. I wondered if Hannah would recognize me, but she reached out with knowing in her eyes. I held her. Her little arms intentionally squeezed my neck. It was the first time she had ever returned my embrace.

That night, the boys piled into my bed. Three sets of eyes looked at me in a row. I asked them if they understood what was happening. Ben and Sam did a pretty good job of explaining Guillain-Barré Syndrome. "Yeah, we know. Dad's nerves were attacked, and now he is paralyzed."

"Well... yes... that's right." I nodded. "It's a weird thing. Sometimes, not very often, the body gets confused and attacks its own nerves. Do you know what nerves are?"

"Not really," they said.

"The nerves are like train tracks running throughout the body. The tracks are how the brain sends messages to the different parts of the body. Messages like 'pick up your feet and walk' or 'wave your hand.'" I checked to see if they were following and then continued. "Do you know what happens when train tracks are damaged?"

"The trains can't travel?"

"Exactly! The trains can't travel. And if the trains can't travel, the body doesn't get the important messages from the brain. Without the messages from the brain, the body can't move. And that, my friends, is why Dad is paralyzed. And since Daddy's train tracks are damaged, we just have to wait for them to get fixed. Once they are fixed, Dad's body will get the message to move again, and while I know it's not easy to wait, we just have to do it."

I apologized for not being home. I apologized for not being there when they needed me most. I explained that I had really wanted to be with them, but Daddy really, really needed me.

Sam asked in a quiet voice, "Is Daddy going to die?"

Knowing this question would come, I responded with my rehearsed answer. "We don't expect that to happen."

March 3, 2019

We left early for Sioux Falls, and our haste made us ahead of time for our scheduled meeting with the Child Life specialists. We sat in the family room visiting with Grandma Barb. The children looked around impatiently.

"So, where's Dad?"

"He's in the ICU," I said. "If you are ready to see him, we can go back to his room. But if you feel a little nervous, we can wait a while too."

"We want to see him," they said eagerly.

Thinking of the plan I had made with the Child Life specialists, I asked, "Do you want a tour of the hospital first?"

"No. We want to see Dad."

"Okay then," I gathered myself. "Let's go."

So much for the plan.

We found Chris waiting when we drew back the curtain. Chad had combed Chris' hair and raised his bed to make it look like he was sitting tall. The children rushed to his side. They gently but diligently worked around the tubes to hug him. Everyone took turns, not disturbed in the least that he was intubated or couldn't talk. As they laid their heads on his chest, Chris closed his eyes and absorbed the love. The muscles in his face tensed with each hug. It was his way of returning the embrace since he couldn't wrap his arms around them.

It didn't take long before they turned into regular children again. They asked a million questions. *What's that machine? Why is that beeping? What does that say?* They watched the blood spin in the plasmapheresis machine with keen interest. They vied over who got to assist Chris as he communicated using the laser light and letter board. They fought for the privilege of recording Chris' selected letters on the dry erase board. *That's not fair... he got to do it last time!*

The other families in the ICU were extremely gracious as our children strutted the halls. Someone commented on how grounding it was to have children there. They added a lighter dimension to the difficult moments. One spunky ICU nurse, the one who could brighten Chris' day by finding ways to recognize his humanity, created peak moments for the children. Her husband worked hospital security, so she lined up a visit to the room where the security cameras played on television screens. After that, the children got to watch the hospital's helicopter depart from the helipad as it was called into action. All in all, a successful day. We left and drove to the hotel.

It was snowing that night, creating white knuckle driving conditions. It had been a good day for the children, but Chris' illness, as well as the intense amount of attention it took to manage four children in the ICU, had me exhausted. Everyone in the car was tired and hungry, including baby Hannah. In the dark, she cried so loudly that her piercing screams cut at our eardrums. Tensions grew until we heard the unexpected sound of a beautiful singing voice coming from the backseat. Pairing the name Hannah to the theme song of the movie *Home Alone*, Ben sang. Hannah quieted, listening. The other boys joined in one at a time. In the dark, the car filled with the sound of my angel choir. My heart burst with love and gratitude.

Adyashanti was right. The miracle of grace can appear when and where we least expect it.

March 5, 2019

I stood by the hospital's main entrance and loaded the children into the car at the end of our weekend together. My dad's steady arm at the helm, I watched them drive away. The loneliness and desperation returned immediately.

Soon after their departure, Chris began to describe bizarre sensations. "You feel like your head is in a cage and your torso is balancing on top of it?" I read his letter board message and looked to him for confirmation. I didn't know how to respond. I couldn't stop the smile forming on my lips. "Oh, umm. Wow. That sucks," I said as my voice trailed off. I didn't have any other words. I squeezed my lips together, waiting for something better to come out, but nothing did. I could hear the ventilator tubes clinking together as Chris shook his head up and down, agreeing that it did, in fact, suck. I wondered if the tiny eye roll accompanying his nod was added for emphasis or if it was meant to imply something else.

He described the feeling of nails and other metal pieces filling his mouth. His jaw falling off. His foot being impaled by a wooden spear... The list went on. The doctors explained that damage to the peripheral nervous system can create phantom sensations in the body. But that provided little direction on how to deal with a husband whose reality was that his torso was balancing on his head while his foot was being impaled with a wooden spear and now had little ability to communicate and needed me to speak on his behalf.

With continued support from Chris' family, I took brief reprieves from the hospital room. I needed time away from everyone to deal with what needed to be done. I checked my work emails, paid bills, cancelled our upcoming Disney trip, and considered options for long term sustainability and back up plans for Chris' business. Working through these details helped me clear the clutter, create a path, and focus on the possibilities. Seeing the possibilities helped me ask the right questions. Asking the right questions helped me make good decisions. This was not an intentional strategy. It was my way of clinging to the edge of sanity.

I spoke with our case manager outside of Chris' ICU room as I looked for ways to orient myself to our potential future. Shine a light on the broader landscape. Take control of this rugged terrain. The position of case manager is one designed to help patients navigate the way through insurance and transitioning care. With her as a guide, I unfolded the map of life. I said, "We know where we are going. Home. We just don't know how we are going to get there yet. We are in the process of charting our route." The case manager nodded, accepting my understanding of reality.

"Like any road trip, there are several ways of getting to the same place. Some routes are shorter, and some are longer. Without a way to see into the future, though, it's hard to know which path we are on. Are we going the short way or the long way home?"

It was a rhetorical question of course, but the long way seemed more and more likely. There had been no real indication of improvement, and Chris would soon undergo surgery for a tracheostomy. The case manager helped me prepare for the long way. "Until Chris can get off the ventilator, he can't begin any major therapy. Not in South Dakota anyway. The rehabilitation center here can't take people on ventilators," she said.

I imagined Chris deteriorating in a hospital or nursing home. Just lying there for several months. Our family members were the ones assisting Chris with his range of motion activities aside from the five minutes he got from a physical therapist each day. We took turns lifting his deadweight legs, rotating his ankles, and stretching his limp arms. We were untrained and guessing at the appropriate amounts of extension. We didn't want to hurt him, but we didn't want him completely immobile either. We would do anything for Chris, but this wasn't a sustainable solution.

The case manager explained that there are rehabilitation hospitals in the country that work specifically with patients who have undergone neurological illnesses and injuries. Even better, some are equipped to accept patients on ventilators. She pointed to the Madonna Rehabilitation Hospital in Lincoln, Nebraska. A facility located seven hours from our home. She asked if I would be interested in talking to an admissions representative from Madonna. At first, it felt drastic to send Chris that far from home, especially with such a young family. But if we were taking the long way home, I had to consider the bigger picture. The reality was that the longer it took Chris to recover, the less chance he had at a full recovery. And the sooner the rehabilitation, the better the outcome. If the ventilator was going to deter us, we would need to find a way to work around it. The sacrifice of having him far from home might actually be an investment in the long run. I agreed to visit with someone from Madonna.

March 6, 2019 | morning

Chris was transferred to the Acute Neurology floor the same day he got his tracheostomy. I gasped when I saw him without the tubes protruding from his mouth. He stretched his jaws as he reacquainted himself with the space between his lips. He smiled when he saw me. I kissed him.

It didn't take long for me to become familiar with the Acute Neurology floor. The coffee pot, snack drawer, ice machine, and bathroom were all near. I could tell that the nurses were skilled in supporting Chris' unique needs. They didn't hesitate before gracefully maneuvering his body to clean him or reposition him to avoid skin sores. They provided good counsel and acted as partners in his care. But while they were mighty helpful, Chris wasn't getting better. His pain skyrocketed and the movement in his shoulders and neck decreased even more. Then he stopped blinking.

Chris' eyes had gradually gotten red and sore looking, but practically overnight the outside layer of skin on his eyeballs had formed a bumpy, leathery texture. He wasn't seeing well either. When he tried to communicate, his laser light wandered aimlessly over the letter board. I requested a consultation with ophthalmology. The ophthalmologist, who in small world South Dakota just happened to be the brother of one of my best friends, examined him. He pulled a mini flashlight from his pocket and asked Chris to follow it with his eyes. When the light moved up and down, left to right, he determined that Chris' eye muscles weren't strong enough to track it. Chris was seeing double. His eyelids, which still fluttered with a blinking motion, were not closing all the way either. The physician said we probably didn't even know when Chris had been sleeping. He instructed us to squeeze a line of ointment into his eyes and then tape them shut to preserve their health. This also meant our communication method was no longer available. While he could still hear us, Chris was now trapped inside his body with no way to communicate.

March 6, 2019 | afternoon

We were required to move out of our ICU family room when Chris was transferred to the Acute Neurology floor, so we set up camp in the community waiting room as an alternative. We rearranged the furniture to make a sleeping area. This created less privacy for everyone in the waiting room, but it worked in the short term.

Chris' only sister, Suzanne, had traveled to South Dakota from California to help. She and I had been dear friends since college. In fact, she introduced Chris to me when I was an undergraduate and he was working toward his master's degree. Since we lived in the dorms at the time, my girlfriends and I would go to Suz's brother's house to socialize. We would listen to Chris' music, eat his food, and then wait for him and his friends to come home so we could hear about the downtown scene. It was a safe and happy place where we made countless memories. It wasn't until a few years later that Chris and I started dating, though.

Suzanne asked how I was doing during a rare moment together in the waiting room. I told her everything. I told her that I was tired. I felt horrible that I wasn't with my children. That I had no way of knowing where we were in this journey or how we would emerge. Chris couldn't move, talk, or see. He was in incredible pain. I felt awful. She let me spill my fears while listening openly and with non-judgment. We ended the conversation on a lighter note. She told me about her frequent travel for work and that she'd learned to rely on a healthy diet and workout plan for balance while away from home. Trying out a bit of humor, I commented on my recent diet plan. "Personally, I have found that the my-husband-suddenly-got-paralyzed diet is quite effective for weight loss, but I wouldn't recommend it." My irreverence made us giggle, even though it wasn't especially funny.

Later in the waiting room, I found Chris' mom swapping health stories with strangers, reminding me of where Chris had inherited his relational personality. She listened to their challenges with a loving ear before sharing ours. I overheard a woman casually respond, "Oh, I worked with someone who had Guillain-Barré Syndrome once. Yeah, it's sad. Years later, he's still in a nursing home, unable to walk."

I hunched over and covered my ears. Rocking back and forth, I yelled, "Laa-laaa-laaa-laaa-laaa," until the woman stopped talking. Even with my hands over my ears, I could hear Barb explain that I was the wife.

Aware of what she had done, the stranger came to my side and sheepishly said, "I hope your husband gets better soon." I wish I had been the bigger person, but I wasn't. I didn't open my eyes or unplug my ears until she left.

7

when

the shoe drops

romance is a matter of perspective

I see you

falling, we go

together but separate

the long way

Mother Mary, pray for us

teach us how to live

the stuff of dreams

reawakened

on the other side of life

the ultimate destination

home

March 6, 2019

Chris got his tracheostomy on Ash Wednesday. At the service in the chapel that morning, I gazed at the crucifix. I saw a man hanging, dangling, and suffering on the cross. A pained and far off expression in his eyes. It was a position of vulnerability, yet it was a position of strength. The physical similarities of Jesus' suffering, limp and pained, jumped out at me. I didn't say anything, but the familiarity was uncanny. Chris' face had become angular and his beard fuller. His hands and feet were in significant pain.

I'm not comparing Chris to Jesus the Christ. *Really, I am not.* What I'm saying is that I will never look at the crucifix in the same way. In that moment, I realized that I wasn't alone. Suffering had new meaning. Suffering is a sand shovel digging a hole deep into my heart. The gravel like friction scraping and stinging with every scoop. But the man affixed to the cross, looking oddly like my husband, symbolized a friend who understood my suffering. He symbolized the water that slowly filled the gaping new hole in my heart.

March 6, 2019 | evening

There was a pull-out couch in Chris' Acute Neurology room. After he was prepared for sleep that night, medications distributed and eyes taped shut, I took my post. The ventilator and heart rate monitor provided white noise. Chris was still, so I stretched my body on the couch and then curled into a ball, trying to get warm under a blanket. My head lay on the plastic pillow I selected only after careful examination. There were many pillows in the room, but most had been used to prop Chris into multiple positions, mopping up various body fluids along the way.

It was dark in Chris' room, but light escaped from the curtained window by the door to the hall. The hustle never stops

in a hospital, and I could sense the activity on the other side.
It made me recall the feeling I had as a little girl in the bedroom
I used to share with my sister. I would lay in bed afraid of the
night, wondering what my parents were doing on the other side
of the door. I could relate to that little girl. I was tired, but I was
scared to sleep in here.

Chris' head jerked toward the call button positioned on
his pillow. His call button was designed for patients with little
mobility. It only required a light tap of his forehead to notify
the nurses and aides that he needed help. He couldn't quite reach
it, though, so I scrambled out of bed to ask what he needed.
I went through the list of common requests. *Reposition? Pain?*
Itch? Bathroom? Cold? Hot? Obviously, I wasn't offering the right
one from the quick shakes of his head. I rearranged the pillow
supporting his neck, and he nodded slightly as if to confirm that
I had addressed the issue. I positioned his call button by his forehead
again and returned to my makeshift nest. Just when I had allowed
my muscles to rest, Chris jerked his head aggressively toward the
call button. I rushed to his side and frantically walked through
the many possibilities again with no success. I could tell he was
frustrated, so I clicked the call button myself and anxiously awaited
the arrival of two aides. They repositioned Chris and checked
the pad under his body to see if he needed cleaning. I lay down.

As soon as they left, Chris jerked his head again. Back by his
side, I pleaded with him. I desperately wanted to help, but I didn't
know what to do. I hit the call button again. He wrestled himself,
violently uncomfortable. I sensed that we were in a fight. I imagined
him angry with me, and I was helpless to know my error much less
correct it. When the aides returned, I sat on the edge of the bed
with my head in my hands. Frantic, dejected, trapped. One aide
sat down next to me, speaking in his soothing accent... Caribbean,

was it? I couldn't see his face. He told me I needed to get some sleep. They would take care of Chris. I should lie down. Completely helpless to the situation, I gave up, lay down, and stayed down, even when Chris continued to struggle. Alone in the room with him, I squeezed into a tight ball with my fists over my ears and pulled the covers over my head.

Hell is as bad as its reputation.

March 7, 2019

Barb and I drove south. We were shell shocked from a long and harried month in the hospital. After being bombarded with constant life threatening issues, it was disorienting to be on the open road, but it was mission critical that we tour the Madonna Rehabilitation Hospitals in Lincoln.

This wasn't our first road trip. Eight years before, Chris, Barb, baby Ben, and I had taken a three week journey through Rocky Mountain, Zion, Yosemite, and Yellowstone National Parks. We'd exclaimed over the scenery as six-month-old Ben snoozed happily in his car seat. A couple years and a couple more children later, we'd ventured through the Grand Canyon, Arches, and then the Grand Tetons. And just a few months earlier, during my maternity leave with Hannah, we traversed Glacier National Park. Now, headed to Nebraska, I leaned back. This was a very different kind of road trip.

Barb was not driving fast. I watched, one after the other, as people passed us in their vehicles. When they got close enough, I searched their faces, wondering what they were thinking and where they were going. Some people chatted on their phones. Others bobbed their heads to music. It was bizarre to know that life had continued as usual for the rest of the world when ours had been blown to pieces. Only a fragment of myself, I tried to remember

what it was like to be normal. I suggested to Barb that we find
a restaurant where we could have a glass of wine and be around
people who were laughing. She tried to appease me once we
were in Lincoln, driving aimlessly to find a place until she finally
turned into an Arby's drive-through to order her usual: two fish
sandwiches. I quickly lost interest in laughing. I spotted a Dairy
Queen on our way to the hotel and asked Barb to pull over so
I could order a banana split. I ate in bed.

March 8, 2019

The next morning, we walked through Madonna's large sliding
glass doors for the first time. The foyer was bright and airy. Very
pleasant, actually. It featured a wall of trickling water with the
Madonna logo displayed underneath. On the opposite wall was
a television that showcased the stories of past patients who had
worked their way back to life. Names of Madonna Foundation
donors were etched into the surrounding stone. I smelled chlorine.
The large therapeutic pool was just around the corner.

The Spinal Cord Injury Program Manager, Diane, greeted
us with a welcoming smile. She had sincere eyes and a reassuring
presence. She acknowledged our difficult situation by saying, "I am
so sorry you are going through this." Then she guided us toward
the elevator, explaining that our tour would follow the same order
in which Chris would use the facility if we decided to come to
Madonna. I was taken by the large and striking painting of Mother
Mary, the Madonna, as we rounded the corner. In the portrait,
she was framed by a glowing veil that fell elegantly down the length
of her back. My eyes lingered on the expression of calm resolve
brushed into her pale, angelic face. I tried to reproduce it on my own.

The elevator brought us to the second level. We walked out
onto the Long-Term Acute Care (LTAC) floor. Diane explained

that the second floor houses patients who need more intensive care like Chris. Most of the patients on LTAC are on ventilators and still recuperating from serious medical issues. When they recover to the point that they can tolerate three hours of rehabilitation per day, they are transferred to the first floor, where the heavy duty therapy takes place. Diane led us down a quiet hallway, a stark contrast to the hustled tension of the ICU and the Acute Neurology floor to which I had become accustomed. As we walked, she explained that Chris would be under medical supervision on LTAC, but he would also have a regular therapy schedule that would include sessions with speech, occupational, physical, and respiratory therapists. But the primary goal for his time on LTAC would be to wean him from the ventilator.

The patient room that Diane showed us was plain but cheery with soft yellow walls, laminate wood floors, and a big window facing the street. The bathroom was distinct from the other hospital bathrooms I had seen. It was exceptionally large. Big enough for a wheelchair to roll into the shower. Diane motioned for me to take a seat in a guest chair. I sat down. I watched as she brought in another chair for Barb and positioned it directly opposite me. She leaned against the windowsill in between us.

Diane was the first person I had met who was even remotely familiar with the recovery from Guillain-Barré Syndrome. Everyone else to this point had only handled the acute part of the syndrome. The deadly part before the recovery. I seized the opportunity to ask her questions. *How long does recovery take after a severe case? What are the chances that Chris will get everything back? If he comes home in a wheelchair, how will I take care of him?* In between these questions, I gave her the context of our lives. I talked about our four young children, our home seven hours away, Chris' business, and that I hadn't been able to work with any regularity for the last month. I found myself flooded with emotion as my repressed fears crawled out of hiding. Essentially, I was asking her what would become of us.

I saw tears pool in Diane's eyes as she listened. She couldn't tell me that everything would be all right. She couldn't tell me that Chris would make a full recovery. She couldn't tell me how long it would take until he was ready to come home. What she could tell me, though, was how the therapists at Madonna would help him prepare for his return. And how I could prepare myself and our home if he required a wheelchair, which was most likely. She talked about disability accommodations and the assistive equipment we might need to install to help with transfers from his wheelchair to the bed. But it wasn't until she started talking about bowel care that the realities of paralysis really set in. I gulped and looked at her. "Bowel care?" I asked in a small voice.

"We try to do suppositories in the morning so the bowels get used to emptying at that time. That way, it will be easier to have a routine for toileting and cleaning when you go home," she answered.

I was no stranger to the messiness of incapacitation. I had been living it up close and personally. But thinking about the routine at home was a gut-punch. There would be no help from the nurses' aides, and I would be juggling the competing needs of four children as I tried to keep Chris clean and dry. I sank deeper into my chair. I was weary. Tired from the trials of the last several weeks. Tired from glimpsing our challenges to come. I finally succumbed to my heavy burden. I stopped resisting it with all my might and instead allowed it to encompass me.

I had put all my focus on Chris until that moment, pushing away the thoughts and questions about how this disease could affect my life and the lives of our children in the future. I had been looking backward, hoping against hope that Chris would return home relatively unscathed after a quick recovery, and we could resume our normal life. But that was a dream, and I was ready to admit it. In the course of my conversation with Diane, I stopped looking backward and, instead, swiveled my head to the future. It was obvious that we were taking the *really* long way home. While it was uncomfortable to hear, I wanted to understand the real possibilities because when the time came to deal with them, I needed to be emotionally ready to set the *can-do* attitude for Chris and the children.

Barb wasn't as open to entertaining these less than ideal possibilities for her baby. She was hell bent on holding out for the very best outcome and quickly dismissed the more dismal realities. She seemed bothered by the acknowledgement of my fears and my resulting surrender. I assumed she was irritated that I had moved past the point where I naturally expected a full recovery, burying that wish in the very back of my mental drawer. Or because I had exposed the less valiant side of my caregiving identity. The side that was scared and selfish and tired.

Barb attempted to inject positivity into the conversation, but it all felt defensive to me. She tried to steer the conversation in the direction of her comfort level, and when that didn't work, she made simmering comments about how she couldn't see the documents Diane was showing me. My quick glances revealed Barb to be squirming uncomfortably, biting her tongue, and doing her best to snub her mounting frustration. I could only imagine the discomfort she was experiencing. It was obvious that her role as mother didn't qualify as next of kin in this scenario. But, while I could appreciate her position, I had to concentrate on mine. This was a discussion I needed to have. There were real repercussions of being the one left to carry the weight of our lives. Information was my friend. I preferred to absorb the shock of it away from my family.

I continued to process the laundry list of possible impacts on our future. There were so many unknowns. I mentioned that friends at home had asked if they should host a fundraiser on our behalf and how I had batted away the offer, expressing discomfort about accepting charity. Diane looked at me with concern. Reading her vibe, I asked, "Could this wipe us out?" She gave me a half nod and a shrug.

"Should I let them do it?"

"Let people help you. If you find you don't use all the funds, take a vacation at the end of this. You are going to need it."

In that moment, as much as it was uncomfortable, I promised myself that I wouldn't say no to help. If there was ever a time I needed it, that time was now.

Continuing the tour, we visited Acute Rehab on the first floor where Chris would go once he was fully weaned from the ventilator. The huge therapy gym in the center of the building was full of special equipment designed to help people relearn to move. Off to the side of the gym was an experiential learning area with a mock grocery store, bedroom, garage, and vehicle. I thought about the many people who had toured this facility with the knowledge that their loved ones were permanently paralyzed. They weren't coming to rehab to return to life as they'd known it before their injury or illness. They were there to learn how to live very differently. Forever. I thought of a couple in my hometown. After diving headfirst into a swimming pool thirty years before, the husband broke his neck and became quadriplegic. Yet he had overcome his disabilities in nearly every way, even becoming a South Dakota Supreme Court justice. He had been paralyzed ever since I had known him, so I never thought much about it. But now my thoughts turned not to him but his wife. I imagined her walking through a similar facility, sick and scared. Her entire life altered in a moment.

My body felt numb in comparison to the explosion of feeling in my heart. It was unbearable. The unexpected realization hit me. We were the lucky ones. While no one knew exactly how Chris' recovery would pan out, we had good reason to hope he would walk again. My eyes welled heavily for all the people who had ever taken this tour, and my tears spilled for those who found themselves with no way back. They streamed down my face and splattered onto my chest.

I took inventory on the drive back to South Dakota. I thought about how the children and I would adjust with Chris seven hours from home. Perhaps I could find a daycare and a summer program for the children and move our family to Lincoln. Maybe I could work remotely. But I decided that walking away from our support system and the children's routines would be more damaging in the long run. Plus, it would be difficult to actually spend time with Chris in the hospital while I kept our four children occupied in a place where they couldn't run.

Barb offered a suggestion as I verbally weighed the options. "I can stay with Chris in Lincoln while you care for the kids at home and get back to work," she said. There was no hesitation in her voice. I knew that it was the best option and was grateful that it existed. Still, it was not an easy decision. It seemed unimaginable for me to walk away from Chris in his time of need. But, as I let it soak in, I came to a quiet conclusion. While it had been extremely difficult to be away from our children, I felt solace knowing that I was being the best mother I could be by taking care of their father. But crossover day was coming. Soon I would need to go home. The best way for me to be a wife would be to take care of our children.

My head and my heart agreed. Chris would go to Madonna. It was the right place.

I asked Chris if he could hear me when I returned to his bedside that evening. His eyes were taped shut, but he gave me a slight bounce of his head. I leaned in and told him about Madonna. I explained that while I preferred he stay in South Dakota, closer to family and friends, I felt that it was in his best interest to start rehabilitation as soon as possible. I laid out my rationale. Madonna had a specialized focus on rehabilitation from neurological issues. It had a legitimate regular therapy schedule for those on ventilators. I had a stellar impression of the staff. Chris seemed far away, but he managed to bob his head slightly in response.

March 9, 2019

We continued to hold vigil while Chris lay motionless. His eyelids snapped wide open when not taped shut. His pain held steady, fluctuating between a nine or ten on the pain scale. One of his physicians sat us down and explained that never in his career had he seen anyone on as much pain medication as Chris. Even though he was still hurting, we needed to start weaning. I chewed my nails nervously, fearing that Chris wasn't ready for this change. I watched his brother bend over and explain the concern to Chris. He whispered into his ear, outlining the plan to slowly cut back. Chris nodded in response. I sighed in relief.

March 1-13, 2019 | CaringBridge journal

I can't believe how busy we are waiting. Yes, I said it. We are *busy* waiting. Our days have been filled with helping Chris communicate his thoughts and needs. Doing passive range of motion exercises with his legs and arms during the day and into the wee hours of the night. Wiping his brow. Icing him when he is hot. Literally blinking his eyes for him, as he cannot currently close them on his own. We are busy talking to the myriad of doctors and therapists as they stop through on daily rounds. We are advocating for Chris and cheering him forward on every level.

Many people fall into the "we" category mentioned above. Chris' mom, Barb, continues to be here every step of the way. Chris' brother, Chad, and sister, Suzanne, who both live in California, have spent weeks with us, which has been an incredible help. Chris' other brothers, David, Billy, and Mike (and their families) have spent their evenings and some overnights supporting Chris and those of us who have been calling the hospital home. My parents have assumed the primary care of our four beautiful children and have created a safe, loving, and stable environment for them until further notice. And my mom, who had already been working with Chris at Maxwell Strategies, has stepped up and continued the charge with her ever professional, experienced, and can-do attitude. They are all heroes, and I (we) will forever be grateful.

Since I shared our last update, Chris not only completed his six sessions of plasmapheresis but also underwent surgery to place his tracheostomy after fifteen days of being intubated. A tracheostomy is a temporary and very welcome step, sometimes referred to as the nurse's best friend because of the patient's enhanced comfort as opposed to tubes in the mouth as well as the easy ventilator trials. These trials allow for testing away from the ventilator, essentially providing the opportunity for the ventilator to be turned off, without the emergent need to re-intubate if the patient continues to need breathing support.

Another big step was that Chris was moved out of the ICU and onto the Acute Neurology floor. We appreciated our time in the ICU as the caregivers were incredible, but Chris is receiving exceptional care on the Acute Neurology floor as well. The nurses in neurology have seen this diagnosis play out in previous cases, and although it feels like a long and weary road now, they assure us that it gets better. They say they have often had the pleasure of seeing their GBS patients tour the floor a year later to see where they'd been while paralyzed.

Another milestone is that our children came to visit for the first time. Chris and I debated whether we should wait until he was extubated; however, we decided to explain the situation to the boys (Hannah being too little) and give them the option of seeing Chris or waiting. The decision was not hard, and they charged right in to see their dad. There were many huge hugs, which Chris thoroughly appreciated and absorbed. Later, the kids got a backstage tour of the hospital with visits to the helipad where they actually saw the helicopter called into action and depart. They also saw the security room where someone monitors the many different areas of the hospital through video surveillance. After the visit, Chris said, "Each of the kids impressed me in their own way." No doubt, this experience will build the concept of resiliency into their characters.

A truly heartwarming experience has been the opportunity to participate in art therapy with the kids. As the kids have made additional visits, a family friend has treated us to art therapy sessions where we have had the opportunity to play, work out our feelings indirectly, and connect. It has been the best experience and highly recommended for kids going through an emotionally challenging ordeal.

In the midst of all of this, in addition to working as best I can, paying bills, keeping tabs on the kids from afar, and trying to partake in normal life activities such as eating and sleeping, we have been getting a fast orientation on rehabilitation options.

Because Chris continues to be on the ventilator, he is not yet eligible for the hospital's in-patient rehabilitation center in Sioux Falls. Nevertheless, his therapy must begin. To that end, Barb and I toured the Madonna facility in Lincoln, where they specialize in rehabilitation from neurologic disorders. The visit was very reassuring, and we look forward to next steps. Chris is currently weaning from certain pain medications and is also being treated for pneumonia. These are things that need to happen before a transfer can occur.

People have said this is a marathon, not a sprint. I am not sure what that means exactly, but I do know that the people around us have been amazing. I have learned that sleep turns out to be necessary. And, I know that in a defining moment such as this when we have little control, we still have a lot of choice. Our choices are limited, sure, but our choices around mental state and attitude are plenty, and making the right choices in these areas makes a big difference. I have had the pleasure of spending the last fifteen years as Chris' wife. During that time, I know Chris has done the mental and emotional work to prepare for this experience. As he does with all things, he will find a way to make this experience *for him*. I can't wait to talk to him about it over coffee. Luckily, we have the rest of our lives for this.

A big shout out to everyone who has helped us in a thousand different ways... You know who you are. We are eternally grateful.

March 19, 2019

Our son Ben had a birthday during the time Chris was transitioning his pain medication regimen. I decided to drive the three hours home to be with him for the evening. Normalcy was delightful, even the family ruckus that played out as my parents prepped the dining room table for pizza, salad, and cake. The shenanigans were the same in good times and in bad. One child poked at the other until he got a reaction. It started with laughter but ended, as usual, with anger. I broke up the scuffle and invited the instigator to spend some time thinking about his choices, alone. Waiting for the timeout to conclude, I sat on the couch. I looked around and wanted to laugh. Sibling drama wasn't really all that dramatic in context.

My phone pinged, announcing a text message. It was from Chris' mom sent to the twelve members of his family on her regular update list. I opened it nervously. It was a picture of Chris lying in his hospital bed. The dry erase board that we'd used to capture his thoughts before we had to tape his eyes shut was propped in front of him. It read, "Happy 9th Birthday, Ben! I love you! From: Dad." Chris was merely the model in the photo, of course. Barb had written the message to remind Ben that his dad loves him. But what was meant to be an affection filled message left me breathless. Chris looked like a corpse. One eye taped shut. His mouth agape. He stared into the distant nowhere. The photo would have frightened anyone, never mind the son of the person in it. I turned off my phone. I had no intention of sharing the picture with Ben. Then, all of a sudden, we were singing *Happy Birthday*, and I swallowed back tears. Ben closed his eyes. His face scrunched into a pained look. He took a deep breath and blew out the candles. We all knew his wish.

March 20, 2019

It was a relief when my friend Jess asked if she could return to the hospital with me. Jess has been one of my best friends since college, but she is also a physician. She had delivered three of my babies. She was no stranger to a hospital, nor was she under any illusions of what she might find when she entered Chris' room. Her husband, the physical medicine and rehabilitation physician who'd helped to diagnose Chris' Guillain-Barré Syndrome, would have shared information about the condition in preparation. Nevertheless, once we arrived at his hospital room, she was surprised. Chris' devastated state was in sharp contrast to the last time she had seen him. She glanced up at me, wiping away tears, and said, "No one at home understands how bad he is. The CaringBridge updates are relatively positive."

Jess transformed into doctor mode. With my permission, she reviewed the case and asked questions about lab numbers and medications. As the physicians performed their daily rounds, we considered new information together. I asked questions and she translated using the medical terms I wished I had known. I was finally able to relinquish my advocacy role, if only for just a little while. Barb, who had not left the hospital except to visit Madonna, went home for a reprieve.

March 21, 2019

We waited for Chris to be medically stable enough for the Madonna transfer. Thinking he had already hit rock bottom, we were surprised when the small movements that remained in his shoulders and neck disappeared. His discomfort was obvious in his intermittent full body sweating, though. He had been getting our attention by bumping the call button positioned by his forehead, but without any motion in his neck, we were now limited to a constant barrage of one word questions. *Pain? Hot? Cold? Readjust?* If the answer was yes, he would stick out his tongue with tremendous effort. He didn't have a way to say *no*.

"So why is Chris' jaw moving like that?" Jess asked, her face screwed into a question mark. I looked at him and hesitated. She was right. His jaw was jumping wildly. I explained that he had been opening and closing his mouth like that ever since the ventilator tubes were removed. At first, I'd thought he was stretching his jaws, a natural response after his mouth had been cranked open for fifteen days before his tracheostomy. But later, the movements correlated with the uncanny phantom sensation of metal in his mouth. On several occasions, he had asked us through letter board communication to search inside his mouth and under his tongue because it felt like a screw or a nail was floating around inside. The constant motion of his jaws had become such a regular movement that I had almost stopped noticing. I stepped back, cocked my head, and took a fresh look. It was indeed odd that every part of his body was paralyzed besides this sporadic, almost involuntarily, chomping. I couldn't believe I hadn't raised the issue before. It definitely wasn't normal.

Jess uttered the words *tardive dyskinesia* as she reviewed Chris' medication list. Tardive dyskinesia is a drug induced condition that causes involuntary jaw movement and, as it turned out, was one of the possible side effects of a certain combination of drugs. A combination that Chris was taking. The condition could be temporary, or it could be permanent. We discontinued the combination promptly, but Chris continued to chomp. It looked like he was gnawing on a bone. I felt sickened by it. Utterly ill. If the twitching was permanent, how would it affect Chris' confidence? Change him as a person? How would he be able to speak to large groups, something he often did for his work, if he couldn't control the movement in his face? The icy hot feeling suddenly returned, making me nauseous. It radiated outward until it prickled my skin. My throat constricted until it felt like I was being strangled. Invisible hands clenched my neck.

Then I noticed another change in Chris. My alarm bells sounded ever louder. Rather than silently struggling, Chris was practically unresponsive.

March 22, 2019

My fears were validated. Chris began to spike intermittent
fevers. Infectious disease physicians prescribed antibiotics
and antivirals. Chris was not medically stable enough for his
transfer to Madonna, so it was delayed. Jess observed me keenly
as I used my breast pump in the corner of Chris' room, no longer
caring about modesty. She listened as I bluntly demanded
that the physician *de jour* talk louder because I couldn't hear
him. It was obvious that I was becoming both impatient and
despondent. She pulled me aside and said, "I think you need to
leave the hospital for a while. I am going to get you a hotel room
so you can sleep. I will stay with Chris. That's why I am here."

I nodded, swallowing hard through the feeling of strangulation.
I needed to leave. It felt so good to have an advocate. Another
friend delivered me to her masseuse for an hour and a half
before dropping me off at the hotel. Then, after an actual meal
at a restaurant, I was in the room. Finally, I was alone in a place
with a lock. Dropping onto the bed, I listened to the stillness.
Being alone also meant that I had no choice but to face myself,
and assessing the damage was uncomfortable. The landscape
of my life loomed in front of me like broken shards of glass.
I picked up my phone several times, but I always put it down
before placing a call. I didn't want to talk to anyone. Not really.
But sitting in bed, surrounded by sweet silence, I felt like I was
going to implode. The tears that seldom came dripped down my
face as I grabbed my computer. I wrote the words I wanted to share
with my husband.

March 22, 2019

Chris, I am so lonely.

I know you are lonely, too. I can't even imagine. And, although I am not in the hospital bed, frozen inside your body, I feel like I can't breathe. I can't move. I feel like my heart is permanently broken, and I can't figure out how to make this better. I am lost. I am dying a little bit more each day. As I write this, I know you are feeling the same way. I am sorry it wasn't me instead. I am sorry you have to take this one. I wish I could take it away.

I am so afraid you are going to be distant and bitter because this didn't happen to me. That I survived somehow. But, honestly I feel abandoned by you. I am alone. I am suddenly alone in this world with the same responsibilities as before but without you. I know you are somewhere in there, deep inside. And yet, you are so far away. I can't find you, and I miss you.

I want to be so strong for the kids. But I don't know what to do or say. I've had to field fundamental questions about life that I am not sure how to answer. "What if Dad dies?"

I haven't cried much, but in this moment when I imagine talking to you, I can't help it. This is so sad. I feel so incredibly sad. I miss talking to you. You are my best friend. I need you. I am not me without you. I want to unload all of this at your feet. I want to divulge the truth of my soul, but, right now, I know this isn't your load to carry. I will carry it alone. Like you do yours.

I have been so sensitive not to irritate you with constant chatter. Noise. I don't want to read you anything for fear it will annoy you. I am fully aware that you are the only one in the hospital room that cannot leave or control anything about your surroundings, so I am figuratively paralyzed by fear that you will secretly hate me for talking to you, trying to entertain you, doing the wrong thing. Yet, I am afraid you will hate me for not talking to you or providing entertainment. I am so afraid. Period. I am mad for not knowing what to do.

How can this be happening? I wake up every day, every hour, and shake myself. Is this really happening, or am I dreaming? How could this be real? Part of me wants to die. But I am so afraid of dying that I don't want to die. I am afraid of the present, and I am afraid of the future. I don't know what to do. I need to be healthier for our kids. They deserve better.

I feel guilty for having feelings of my own. I want to honor your feelings, so I feel guilty if I honor mine. I feel guilty for working. I feel guilty for parenting. I feel guilty if I smile. I feel guilty if I am too exhausted to go into your hospital room. I feel guilty for paying bills. I feel guilty for helping you and, in turn, not even thinking about, calling, or hugging the kids. I am angry that I have to choose one over another. What do I do? Should I be with you, or should I be with them?

I am scared of what I don't know.

When I sit by your bedside, I look desperately for how I can help you, satisfy you for one moment. I want to communicate. I look for any remnant of our relationship. I anxiously look for a shred of *us* in your eyes. Instead, I see pleading. For something. Something I should know you need. When I ask if you want to talk through the letter board, I secretly hope that you will tell me something that lets me know I make you happy. Selfish, probably. But I want to know you love me. I want to know we are okay. I want to know you are giving the kids a message that they are loved and being thought about.

It's asking too much. I know you are at a place of basic needs only. How can I expect you, being as sick as you are, to make me feel better? I feel sick. Heartsick. I feel like I am a dog sitting by my owner. Waiting. Waiting for the directions that never come. I am listening so hard, but I am not hearing anything. And I think I am disappointing you for not following those silent directions, nevertheless. I am sorry.

And, yes, I can hear you say, "Don't apologize."

March 23, 2019

Jess gave me the status report the next morning. She told me that Chris experienced *bradycardia*, an abnormally slow heart rate, during the night. The cardiac event caused his monitor to scream frighteningly. "Honestly, I am glad you weren't here," she said. My inner voice agreed.

Looking for a reality check later that day, I tucked myself into the bathroom of Chris' hospital room holding a piece of paper given to me by a nurse on the Acute Neurology floor. The paper displayed the name and number of a past Guillain-Barré survivor. I placed the call and then introduced myself when it was answered. I asked the past patient if she would be willing to tell me her story. I listened carefully as she described her illness. The similarities were uncanny. While I understood that no two cases of Guillain-Barré Syndrome are alike, this woman's experience very much mirrored Chris'. They were both diagnosed near President's Day weekend in February. They both had extremely severe cases. This person even went to Madonna for her rehabilitation seven weeks after she was initially admitted to the hospital. Ironically, this was the same time frame we were expecting for Chris' transfer. I began counting on my fingers after the woman told me that she had returned home in a wheelchair roughly six months after her diagnosis. If their cases continued to run parallel, Chris might be home in August.

The call helped me regain the tiniest inkling of control, which was good because it was time for Jess to leave. I reflected on the gift she had given me. She had shown up as a partner, a medical advocate, a counselor, and, most importantly, a friend. We've always been real with one another, even to the point of disagreement, but I was left speechless by her show of raw friendship. Friendships are mirrors, and Jess helped me remember who I am. But while identity is found in friendship, it is also found in struggle. Struggle is when you learn what you are really capable of. Unlike friendship, however, struggle is often a lonely venture. Like a fatigued marathon runner is energized by those cheering from the sidelines, Jess gave me a much needed boost. She left me with a thought. "You are the captain of this ship. The captain can't go down. Take care of yourself."

March 14-23, 2019 | CaringBridge journal

It's amazing what you can do when you don't have a choice. That's my response when people say things like, "You are an inspiration" or "I don't know how you are managing everything."

The fact of the matter is that we don't have a choice. Sometimes the road of life just takes a turn, and all you can do is veer your proverbial steering wheel to stay on the road and not total out. It's not comfortable. It's hella scary. And it is the only choice we have.

I am not one to get too much into the details because the daily ups and downs of the hospital are just that. They are dramatic and less meaningful than the bigger trend, so why bring everyone along on the less meaningful and, frankly, horrific part of this journey.

If I was being honest, though, I would tell you that the ups and downs make my chest tight and my heart break. It is difficult to see my amazing Chris Maxwell not able to move, talk, or even blink his eyes. Hence eyelids taped shut to preserve them. That coupled with scary drops in heart rate, unexplained fluctuations in temperature, my guy writhing in paralyzed pain, is enough to make me question my sanity. I feel guilty, constant guilt that I am not the one in the hospital bed having to bear the same kinds of aches and pains. I feel guilty that I can physically wrap my arms around the kids, and he can't.

Anyone who knows Chris knows he is amazing, and I am not saying that just because he is my husband. Chris continues to be amazing. Truly, he seems to be rolling with the punches like a superhero. That said, I know he is lonely and scared. This relational, love filled, big thinker... just... frozen. He is currently stuck in his body and is hardly able to communicate with, much less see, the people standing right next to him. Can you imagine? I am here every day and cannot, however hard I try, imagine the loneliness and frustration he must feel.

I keep picturing an image in a cartoon I have seen. I know you have seen it, too. It's the one where a character is walking across a rickety rope bridge, taking one careful step in front of the other. I feel like I am on that bridge. I am taking one careful step in front of the other, navigating the sway and lack of sturdiness under my feet. Occasionally, one of the unstable boards breaks and I fall, only to catch myself on the ropes before I go down. My vision is not working correctly either, and I can only see a few feet in front of me. I don't know how far across that bridge I have gone. When will I be to the other side?

Where is Chris in this picture? Chris didn't get to walk on the bridge. Instead, he took a crash to the bottom of the ravine.

I know he is down there. He is shouting at the top of his lungs to tell me something, but I can't hear him. We both know we need to keep going, walking, fighting, until we can finally be back together again. He has to find his way back up. I need to direct myself onward.

And the kids? Where are they? Sometimes I feel like I am carrying them on my back. Sometimes, I just don't know. Yet they always have stable ground with my mom and dad (thank you).

The point? This is scary. We miss each other. And we need to keep going.

We are waiting for the green light to transfer to the Madonna rehab facility in Lincoln, Nebraska. We were scheduled to go on Thursday, but something just didn't feel right, so we decided to keep him here in Sioux Falls. I am glad we did, as he has had some additional care for fevers and changes in heart and oxygen rates. Things that should be sorted before sending him on the open road.

I have been lucky enough to have our incredible friend Jess Rasmussen here with us this week. She and many other angels have been caring for both Chris and me, as it seems that both of us need some care. To say that her and her husband Dan's friendship, medical knowledge, doctor talk, and lay person translation has been helpful feels insufficient. It has been beyond helpful.

This week I have had the opportunity to connect with other GBS patients and spouses who were cared for at Avera McKennan Hospital over the last few years. Hearing their stories and knowing they are now on the other side has been comforting.

It was a gift that they were willing to share, as I can imagine it is uncomfortable to be sucked back into what seems to be a distant nightmare. We are not the only ones who have traversed this rocky life detour. They remind me that this is not a dead end.

I just want to emphasize that although some people may fear that paralysis could pair with a vegetative state, this is most definitely not the case here. To demonstrate, although Chris cannot speak with his voice, he has been able to communicate through different methods including pointing a laser light at a letter board. These types of communication methods are not easy. In fact, they are painstaking at times. That said, Chris recently authored the following message through the laser and letter board.

"Success starts with patience, persistence, positivity, proactive action, passion, purpose, planning, process, and knowing that your perfection will come in imperfect ways and at imperfect times."

Wow. Now that's a message worth writing.

8

when

the shoe drops

romance is a matter of perspective

I see you

falling, we go

together but separate

the long way

Mother Mary, pray for us

teach us how to live

the stuff of dreams

reawakened

on the other side of life

the ultimate destination

home

I spent a sleepless night Googling *tardive dyskinesia* and taking silent stock of our life to come. I envisioned a heartbreaking future with Chris struggling against himself, trying to hold his head high while also trying to hold it steady. I visualized him bending down to kiss our sweet baby, only to have his jaw jerk around wildly, unable to rest his lips on her soft skin. My emotions tumbled from worry to hopelessness to desperate anger and then back to worry. I paced. I tossed and turned. I nearly burst with unshed tears.

Seeing Chris the next morning only deepened my dread. He was a skeleton. The putrid smell of feces, sweat, bacteria laden mucus, and antiseptic lingered in the air. His jaws gnashed and twitched over his wrecked and paralyzed body. The grotesque movement was all I could see with my eyes open or closed. A sour taste in the back of my mouth. I was in the depths of despair.

An unexpected turn. My phone rang. It was our case manager calling to let me know that Chris would be transferred to Madonna that day. In fact, it would happen within the hour. The contract ambulance service was on its way. It was Monday. I hadn't expected a transfer to take place until Tuesday at the earliest. I jumped into high gear, ready to end this chapter of our lives and turn the page.

Chris' many physicians stopped by, one after the other, before his departure. I visited with them outside of his room as we addressed the transition of care. I reiterated my fear about tardive dyskinesia. The neurologist said he had been monitoring Chris' facial movements and was not concerned at this time. I felt the weight lift with these words and practically floated away. With a childish giddiness, I said, "If I didn't think people would look at me strangely, I'd dance a jig right now. I have been so worried."

Barb and I hastily collected our belongings from the room, once again loading everything into plastic bags. We had collected cards, remnants of care packages, a backpack filled with coloring books for the kids, and the blankets we had used on the floor of the ICU waiting room. When the ambulance service arrived, it didn't take long to figure out that the paramedics were not well accustomed to working with quadriplegics. Barb and I watched with concern, cringing when Chris' head banged against the metal corner of the stretcher as they pulled him from his bed. We described Chris' needs and outlined his preferences as if we were first time parents giving instructions to a new babysitter. We described the subtle things Chris did to communicate, and we provided a list of possible translations. The paramedics looked at us, blinking. They listened but their nonverbals said, "Yeah, yeah, ladies. No problem. Now get out of the way and let us do our jobs."

The paramedics briefed Chris on what to expect during the trip. They warned him that he may not be very comfortable because the stretcher was hard and the ambulance bumpy. The mobile ventilator would feel different, too. "Think of the hospital ventilator as the Cadillac. The ventilator you'll be using for the trip might feel more like a Geo Metro."

I imagined Chris' sarcastic response. "Thanks fellas. That makes me feel a lot better." But I knew his positive side would take over. I practically heard him say, "As long as it drives."

The paramedics circled Chris' body when they finished with the ventilator, cinching the straps that secured him to the stretcher. I followed behind, protectively smoothing his body parts from the resulting crunch. Then Barb and I worked to prepare Chris' eyes for the trip as the paramedics stole glances at their wrist watches. I squeezed a healthy dose of lubricant into his eye before pinching his eyelashes with both thumbs and pointer fingers. I pulled his top lid to carefully overlap his bottom one. Barb maneuvered around me as I held the lid closed. Starting at the corner of his eyebrow, she placed a strip of tape at an angle and laid it gently over the closed eye, allowing me to remove one hand. She then positioned another strip of tape at the opposite corner of his eyebrow and smoothed it diagonally over the lid until it met the other piece at his cheekbone. I removed my other hand. Barb rubbed the tape, coaxing it to hold tightly. I spread the last piece of tape horizontally from the inner to outer corners of the eye to ensure a good seal.

Much to our dismay, his eyes wouldn't stay shut no matter how many times we reapplied. The muscles in his eyelids contracted so violently that they would break free from the tape and snap right back into place, giving him a frightened (and frightening) wide-eyed look. His sweaty skin, mingled with the lubricant, didn't help. I thought back to the ophthalmologist who had recommended that we stitch his eyes shut. I might have considered it, but Chris' opposition had been clear. He had given me a please-don't-sew-my-eyes-shut look.

Neither Barb nor I would be traveling in the ambulance. Barb needed her vehicle in Lincoln, and I had to return home to watch the children as my parents were staffing an out-of-town event for Chris' business. Frustrated, we gave in to the fact that his eyes would have to remain open. The paramedics would be responsible to lubricate and blink them on their four-hour trip to Lincoln. We prayed they would remember. It was easy to forget how frequently a person blinks.

My body shaking, I walked to the departure area where they loaded Chris into a pink ambulance. I had never seen a pink ambulance before, but stranger things had happened in the last several weeks. Chris had not been without a family member for more than a few minutes during his time at the hospital, so it was bizarre to think that we were sending him out onto the open road with only a portable ventilator to breathe and two strangers to manually blink his eyes. This was trust in its most basic form. The ambulance drove away. I felt hollow.

I walked back inside to gather the last of our things and say goodbye. Barb was reviewing the directions given to her by the paramedics. A very wet spring, the Missouri River had already begun its flooding and many of the usual roads between Sioux Falls and Omaha were closed. I thanked Barb for her devotion. I couldn't adequately capture in words my appreciation for her willingness to remain with Chris in Lincoln. She was making it possible for me to be with my babies again. We hugged in the empty room. Mother to mother.

March 25, 2019 | afternoon

I loaded my things into the car and closed the trunk. I sat in the driver's seat for a moment of silence before turning on the vehicle. We had been in this hospital for forty days. Now, I started the engine and wound my way through the familiar parking garage one last time. Nothing more than that. I drove away.

The quiet ride home was one of jubilation. I was going home to be with my children. While this was far from over, we had survived the first horrendous phase of Chris' disease. I received a call that Chris had arrived in Lincoln safely at about the time I pulled into town. He was settling into his new room and getting adjusted after the long ride. The paramedic on the phone said the transfer had been relatively uneventful. No major disruptions. When Barb was reunited with Chris, she gave me a positive report as well. I asked if his jaw still moved erratically. She took silent inventory and said it seemed to be slowing down. I sent up a quiet prayer of thanks.

Friends delivered dinner to my parents' house that evening. Individually wrapped burritos, salsa and chips, Mexican beer, and a large vase of lilies. The children were surprised to see me, but they were even more surprised after dinner when I told them to pack their bags. We were going home. We needed to return to our life. Figure out how to live without Daddy.

Back home, the house felt stagnant. But the air began to circulate as soon as the children resumed their never-ending game of chase and everyone's bags were hauled to their bedrooms. By the time my parents left us for the evening, everyone had taken their baths and the baby was tucked into her crib. The three boys jumped into bed with me and talked as the lights went out. The little voices dropped off one by one, and I smiled in the dark.

March 26, 2019

Returning to our life meant getting the older children to school, the younger children to daycare, and myself to work early the next morning. I was determined to do this with style, so I selected high heels and red lipstick as I got ready for the day. I watched the children breathe effortlessly in bed and swept my fingers over their soft cheeks before I woke them tenderly. I felt accomplished when everyone had dressed, eaten their cereal, and brushed their teeth. We were loaded into the car with plenty of time to spare.

Not sure how to act, I went for casual. When I saw other people, I waved. No big deal, just being normal over here. On the inside, I was jumping up and down while clapping. I breezed into work, and briefly greeted my co-workers as I walked down the hall to my office. I decided the best approach was to compartmentalize. Work was work. Family was family. It would do no good to sit at my desk and mope. Anyway, it felt good to drink coffee at my computer and listen to the idle chatter in the hallway. The problems we solved in my workplace weren't life or death. I loved it. That said, I hated not being in the know about Chris' new environment. My plan was to video conference into his hospital room at various times throughout the day to get updates and visit with physicians.

Barb called at the designated time, and I closed my office door. She showed me Chris lying in his new hospital bed. His room looked bright and cheerful. I saw the respiratory therapists standing next to him performing their routine therapy on his tracheostomy. They affixed a small plastic attachment with tubing that ran from the hole in his neck to an assistive device. The therapist shimmied the tube down his trachea, suctioning mucus like a vacuum cleaner as it traveled toward his lungs.

I was listening intently as Barb described Chris' schedule for the day when the tone and tenor of the room changed drastically. I brought the phone closer to my face as I watched the therapists around Chris become tense as a screeching sound violated the peace. More people rushed into view. I could vaguely hear orders dealt one after the other. Chris looked stiff, his face eerily pale and far away. Suddenly, Barb's face emerged on the screen, and I watched a sharp angle of her chin bob up and down as she was ushered out of the room.

Chris had coded.

I loosened the grip on my coffee mug and set it down. A pit formed in my stomach, and a wave of nausea rushed over my body. I was helpless. Farther away than ever. Barb's phone disconnected and I lay my head on my desk, glad my office door was closed. Barb called back with Chris' physician a few minutes later. Chris had stabilized. They told me that the most likely reason for this scary event had been a *vagal response*, an automatic response of the vagus nerve when it becomes stimulated. The physician explained that it can happen when the tracheostomy is being suctioned, triggering a dysfunction of the heart rate and blood pressure regulating mechanism. It was probably nothing to worry about, but Chris' care team would include a cardiologist going forward.

We will take two, I thought. *One for me and one for him.* I took a sip of lukewarm coffee. It was hard to swallow. My bravado gone, all I could do was stare at my high heels. I couldn't decide if they were silly or appropriate considering the circumstances. Luckily, this bump in the road was small.

March 24–April 2, 2019 | CaringBridge journal

We had a big change last week. We were preparing for a move to Madonna on Tuesday, but early Monday morning it was clear that Chris was ready to go. Elation! We are moving this show on the road to recovery. A flurry of activity. Last visits from physicians and nurse managers. Goodbyes to the different people who had become friends in this less than ideal experience. Even in his compromised state of reality, Chris had found his way into the hearts of many. I remember one time in the ICU when a patient technician had come into Chris' room and asked if he needed anything. Chris shook his head *no* and then indicated he wanted to write. He spelled out, "How are you?" That sweet woman never looked at Chris the same.

Getting him ready for the transfer involved a team of many people. The team transferred him onto a special cot that fit the ambulance. Then they transitioned him from the hospital ventilator to a portable version and prepped his medications. We described the many things we knew he preferred and needed as well as how he communicates. When they wheeled him out of his hospital room, Barb and I looked at each other. Another empty room and another transition. But this time, it wasn't a trip to the ICU.

Emerging from the parking garage of the hospital, I felt untethered. The place I accidentally kept referring to as the "hotel, I mean hospital" was no longer our home. Chris wasn't there anymore. My heart wasn't there. Instead, my heart was speeding down the road in a pink ambulance headed for Lincoln, Nebraska, while I... well... drove the opposite direction. Counterintuitive. I was headed home where our kids needed me because they didn't have care for the week. Intuitive. A tangle of emotion.

The first few days in Lincoln were difficult. As we were forewarned, the transfer was hard on Chris, and he was exhausted. There were so many new people and new processes as well. However, a few days into it, he looked like a totally different person. Not only was he wearing a t-shirt and shorts and had gotten his beard trimmed, but he was mentally sharper than he had been in the week and a half preceding the move.

At home, I felt worlds away but was able to FaceTime into the first few days of therapy sessions. One day, Barb called, and I got to see Chris in a wheelchair with a big smile on his face. This literally brought a gasp to my throat and tears to my eyes.

And now, the really good news. This week, we have seen things that help us know we have turned the corner. The first thing happened when his occupational therapist was working with him. She coached, "Okay, Chris, pretend that your mom is feeding you something you do not want to eat." He pursed his lips which evoked an eye squint and, voila, a blink. He was able to close both eyes on his own. Although not instinctive yet, he can intentionally blink. A big deal.

Even better, I witnessed something miraculous happen when on FaceTime with Chris and Barb earlier this week. The two had worked out that he was feeling nauseous, so Barb asked if his stomach hurt. All of a sudden, we saw movement in Chris's torso. His stomach was pushing in and out. We stopped breathing and looked at each other. The nurse who happened to be in the room at the time questioned whether this movement was intentional, so Chris stopped. We asked him to move again, and he was able to push his stomach in and out. From there, he tested out other movements, which proved mobility in his trunk. At this moment, he is able to swivel his head, shrug his shoulders, move his stomach muscles, and wiggle his hips. Hallelujah and amen! Regaining movement is one of those things that may come and go a bit before it sticks, but it has been there consistently for the last few days and counting.

Through this process, I have learned that what is here today isn't necessarily there tomorrow. And isn't that true for life? So, I am going to choose gratitude for today's small things. For what feels like long lost movement. For Chris' smile that can light up a room and make you feel safe all at the same time. For the ability to be a mom. To hug, play, and run the kids around from activity to activity. To see and savor each child's individual personality. For our three-year-old, Isaac who speaks adorably in the third person. "Isaac wants to do that" or "What about Isaac?" For the ability to truly appreciate my baby girl as she acts out "soooo big" for audiences and parrots the classic "uh, oh" for the first times.

I realize that in our normal life, we get to choose the way we spend our days. We get to choose the daily events that turn into pattern, routine. Heading toward recovery, I want to be careful of what I take with me on the journey back to normal. I want to be intentional about what I pack in my luggage. As I begin this process of selection, I know that I choose vibrant joy, trust, and the power of knowing that I get to (not *have to*) do the things that create my life.

By the way, my homecoming felt like I was falling into the arms of the most loving community. I am reminded of the time I literally fell into the arms of the junior high principal who'd just happened to be standing there when I crossed the finish line of the 400-meter dash in ninth grade track.

My family and friends continue to teach me how to be a better human. Thank you for your example.

April 6, 2019

My parents, the children, and I were back in my white minivan headed to Lincoln the first Friday night after my return home. I was sandwiched between Isaac and Sam in the backseat as I doled out fruit snacks, played peek-a-boo with Hannah, and read books to Ben. The road closures were in full force due to the high waters of the Missouri, so we slowly moved through Nebraska as we navigated state and county roads in the black night. I could hear my parents squabbling in the front seat as my dad questioned the GPS directions. We arrived at two o'clock in the morning.

Later that morning, we walked through the automatic doors of Madonna. The sun streamed through the big lobby windows. The children ran ahead, eagerly searching the area. They climbed onto the water feature and sought permission only after they'd already dipped their little hands into the water. I *shhhh*-ed loudly as their shrieks echoed down the hallway. We lingered by the elevator, examining the pictures and stories of past patients displayed on the wall next to the Lady Madonna portrait. We smiled and said "hello" as current patients rolled by in their wheelchairs.

Ben excitedly told anyone who would listen that he was there to see his dad.

This hospital felt different than the last. Even with its high tech, therapeutic gym equipment, Madonna felt comfortable, like a home. It was cozy and upbeat even though I knew the patients there were dealing with extreme challenges. Pride welled within me as I watched my mom and dad give each other approving glances.

On the second floor, Chris was still hovering at rock bottom, sixty pounds lighter than normal and not able to engage. But his pain seemed under control, and the constant gnashing of his jaws had tempered. I let out a whistle of relief, thrilled to have avoided a collision with tardive dyskinesia. I could tell from the way the staff talked to him and anticipated his needs that neurological issues, paralysis, and ventilators were clearly their specialty. I felt a new sense of security.

I noticed immediately that Chris was wearing a Madonna issued t-shirt and shorts rather than a gown. It was a heartening reminder of normalcy. He was wearing adult size diapers, too, though his catheter tube still ran out the side so his urine could drain into a bag hooked to the bed. This simple thing, something they hadn't used in Sioux Falls, was very welcome. Although diapers might have seemed humiliating at one time, they were cleaner, more dependable, and less embarrassing in the long run. Chris' eyes remained taped shut for the majority of our visit, but when they were open, he was able to look through a prism secured to the lens of his glasses that had been prescribed by Madonna's in-house optometrist. The prism combatted his double vision, something not unusual when the eye muscles are weak.

Barb gave us the tour from the caregiver's perspective. She showed us the pull-out couch in Chris' room where she'd been sleeping. She walked us past the family shower room in the basement and pointed to the hallway that led to an outdoor playground. When we returned to the second floor, she showed us the community snack area. Thrilled by this discovery, the boys took liberties with the available chocolate milk and cookies. Barb introduced us to her new friends that she had made at Madonna as the children ate their snacks in the common area outside of Chris' room. If I had any lingering doubt that Chris had inherited his social nature from his mother, it was gone now.

With the children entertained in the common area, I tended to Chris and observed his new routine. Physicians came in and out as they made their rounds, but it wasn't long before I understood the hierarchy of care. On the Long-Term Acute Care (LTAC) floor, respiratory therapists reigned. They entered the room like clockwork, performing their regular maintenance and determining whether the ventilator settings should be adjusted. I visited with a consulting physician at the door as I watched the therapists work. He said, "Guillain-Barré is kind of a fun disease." I looked at him sideways. *Really?* He crossed his arms and continued. "You see a patient look like this," he unraveled his arms to motion at Chris, "so debilitated… but give it time. Most of them bounce back. It's amazing, really."

Welcomed words.

April 7, 2019

Hannah screamed for several hours on the way home. She filled her diaper so completely that its contents crept up her back and into her hair. Luckily, we had already planned a stop in Sioux Falls. We had tickets to the Harry Potter Symphony at the Washington Pavilion that afternoon, a previous commitment with Ben's orchestral group. Chris' brother David and his wife, Haylee, lived in Sioux Falls. We stopped at their house to run a load of laundry and bathe our poop-covered girl. They generously offered to keep Hannah and Isaac while the rest of us attended the symphony with Ben. I had to convince Sam to join us. But after the first song, he leaned over and whispered, "Whoa, we are lucky. Isaac is really missing out, right?"

I closed my eyes and listened to the crescendos and decrescendos of the strings. My head pounded. Stealing a glance at the boys, though, I sighed with gratitude. Both were sitting on the edge of their seats, their eyes sparkling. With grand gestures, Ben was waving his arms around wildly. He was pretending to conduct the orchestra. Art in the midst of chaos. A calm in the storm.

9

when

the shoe drops

romance is a matter of perspective

I see you

falling, we go

together but separate

the long way

Mother Mary, pray for us

teach us how to live

the stuff of dreams

reawakened

on the other side of life

the ultimate destination

home

Early April 2019

My three boys ran around me in circles as I sat on the floor nursing Hannah. I surveyed my home wearily. Boxes were shoved into corners, and pictures leaned haphazardly against the walls. We'd still been getting settled when Chris got sick, having moved into our house only a year earlier and then getting pregnant with our fourth child shortly thereafter. With two fewer adult hands, I wanted the house to help me, not hold me back. I couldn't waste precious time and energy digging through piles. Everything needed to be organized in a thoughtful, efficient manner.

I told my friends that I needed to make my house a well-oiled machine. My friend Kim asked immediately if I would be willing to delegate the house project to her. I nodded gratefully, surprised by her generous offer. I was filled with newfound energy as we looked through my cupboards, shelves, nooks, and crannies. Kim asked how we used our spaces and what I liked and didn't like. She was ripe with ideas. She said she would gather a team and whip our place into shape, no problem.

Another godsend was the meal train organized by a friend and neighbor. The meal train took the stress of meal planning and preparation off of my to-do list for the first few months after my return. Warm food and a smiling face awaited me every other weekday when I arrived home after work. It was during one of these April meal deliveries that I remembered the message I'd received in the hospital bathroom. *The other side.* At first, I thought it was mystical but later reduced it to the desperate search for hope. I described my experience to our friend delivering the meal. She listened and then asked, "Have you read the book *Falling Upward* by Father Richard Rohr?" She had my attention. Richard Rohr was one of Chris' most beloved authors, but I had not read the book. Our friend explained that *Falling Upward* was about the two halves of life and how, in the words of the author, "The heartbreaks and disappointments of life are steppingstones to spiritual joys that the second half of life has in store." In his book, Father Richard Rohr explains that only those who have gone down, or fallen, can truly understand up. And in that instant, it made sense to me. *The other side* message I'd received signaled our fall into the other side... *of life*. The miracle of grace *can* appear when and where we least expect it.

The many angels in my life rendered me speechless, from leading me to deeper insights, shoveling snow, giving the children rides to and from their activities, unexpectedly fixing our roof when a tree fell on it, and more. I had never been exceptional at gift giving myself being that my love language is quality time, so I marveled at the intricate tapestry our community wove with their threads of kindness. Being close to suffering is uncomfortable, but these people tended to us anyway. They wrapped us in their arms.

And if that wasn't enough, my parents never left my side. My dad's daily routine was to come to my house at six forty-five in the morning to usher the children to the kitchen table for cereal, tie their shoes, and encourage teeth brushing. He loaded the big boys into his pickup truck to deliver them to school on time. I waved goodbye as I loaded the littles into my van, and Isaac and I told funny stories on the way to daycare. At night, both my mom and dad would show up at my doorstep ready to do whatever was needed. They washed dishes, tidied the house, bathed the children, and then tucked us into bed. All this while my mother was pulling double duty working at Chris' business to ensure the trains ran on time in his absence there, too.

I felt loved by them and everyone who surrounded us. Their support gave me the greatest gift, more time for the people who matter most: Ben, Sam, Isaac, and Hannah. I felt like the luckiest unlucky person in the world. I was scared, lonely, and anxious, but I was supported in every possible way.

The weekend we would have been at Disney World, we were back in Lincoln instead. I dropped off my parents and the two youngest children at the hotel before Ben, Sam, and I went to Madonna to say "hello" and "goodnight" to Chris and Barb. As we walked toward the sliding glass entrance, I was filled with the hope of spring. The weather was temperate and the evening air felt soft on my skin. It smelled like fresh flowers. I noticed the same sweet smell as soon as I entered Chris' room. His window was open, and in the dusky evening light, I could just make out the delicate white flowers of the tree blossoms outside.

Chris was sitting in an electric wheelchair, a wonderful change after only seeing him horizontal the last several months. His wheelchair was fully equipped with myriad gadgets and levers, but it also had safeguards to keep his body parts in place. There were guards on the outsides of his thighs, holding his legs steady. His arms were placed in the indents of his armrests and his hands lay atop blue sticky pads so they didn't slip. Chris was still skeletal. His skin lay flaccidly over his bones, but he looked more alive. There was a pinkish hue to his skin. His facial expressions were slightly more dynamic than the previous week, which was enough to be reassuring.

Ben and Sam visited with Chris shyly, uncertain of how to interact. Because he couldn't speak in response, they did their best to carry the conversation themselves, at times looking to me for help. They decided to tell him jokes, a good strategy for one sided conversation. After only a few minutes, they exhausted those they remembered from their milk cartons at school so tried creating a few originals. Their jokes didn't make sense, but we laughed to applaud their creativity and bravery. When Sam took it a step too far, Chris instinctively tried to discipline. He mouthed the words to an unheard reprimand. It was a good sign that he was coming back to life, but his bony face and slow to blink eyes were screwed into a frightening look of disapproval. It appeared as if he was shouting.

Sam, who had missed his dad something fierce, got quiet and shrunk around the corner. I could tell he was still upset when we left the hospital. I explained that it's Daddy's job to tell the kids when their behavior goes over the line. He was just trying to do his job. I reminded Sam that his dad was still very sick, so it wouldn't be surprising if he lost his temper sooner than usual or even looked scarier than intended. "Sam, I bet it hurts your heart to think you might have disappointed Dad, especially when you've been missing him so much." Sam confirmed this with a pained expression. "Daddy loves you, honey. We just need to be patient." He hung his head.

My father received a call the next morning as we ate at the hotel's continental breakfast. I watched as he removed himself from the table and listened intently. I sensed something serious, so I implored him with my eyes to share the reason for the call. When he returned to our table, he said, "Well, it looks like we may have some flooding to deal with this spring." My heart sank. Our community is built on the banks of the Missouri river. Eight years prior, many in our community including us had been displaced by flooding. In an effort to save as much as we could, we moved everything out of our homes, even the kitchen sink and cabinets. The thought of dealing with flooding again on top of our current challenge made me want to vomit.

I nodded and asked, "What's the plan?" He didn't respond.

We spent the majority of the weekend balancing quality time with Chris against the task of keeping the children occupied and the rising anxiety of potential flooding stifled. Quality time with Chris was harder than I'd imagined. With his one eye taped shut, Chris and I attempted to communicate using the laser and letter board again. I diligently wrote each letter as he pointed to it until he would stop abruptly mid-message. I would repeat his name over and over again until he would snap to attention, and we would try again. Finally, when I thought we were in a good flow of communication, I opened my heart to him. I explained how much I'd missed him. I spoke of the children and how they were managing. I described how I was coping in his absence. Desperate for a real connection, I felt a rush of comfort as I spoke. It was so familiar. But, when I looked for a glimpse of acknowledgment in his eyes, he stared straight through me. Then a look of fear struck his face, and I reflexively glanced over my shoulder to search for the cause. Eerily, I found nothing. I begged him for an explanation. Nothing. He didn't even seem to register that I was standing right in front of him. He was somewhere else. Seeing things I couldn't see.

I was uncomfortable. Downright scared. I had allowed myself to be vulnerable with Chris for just a moment. I had hoped for little more than a quick nod of understanding. Fear had been unexpected. Ironically, we were together but more separate than ever. I wondered if he had suffered brain damage. Damage that wasn't detectable until now. Resentment started to bubble, but I stuffed it down as far as I could. It wasn't a logical response. It wasn't Chris' fault he was sick.

I was irritable on the drive home. I screamed at the children as they screamed at each other. I screamed at my dad as he grumbled about having to go through two separate fast food restaurants to satisfy everyone. While I expressed them with irritability, my feelings were stacked in complicated layers.

My physical body was weary. It felt like I was wearing weighted clothing. The next layer was hot with anger, irritation, and panicked madness. I sizzled and burned. Further inward were the feelings of fear. It was where the terrified little Molly hid under her blanket of rage. And finally, there was my core. The core was a pool of calm waters. It was deep knowingness that invited me to enter. This center place kept me upright. It had a voice that calmed me when I was quiet enough to listen. *There, there,* it said.

We arrived home a few hours later to find every light in the house on. The twinkling patio lights crowned three little girls sitting on my front porch swing. Their momma was visible through the front door. She was holding two glasses of wine, waiting. The children hopped out of the car with whoops of excitement. I followed. The front door opened, and we were greeted with hugs. Kim, her husband Matt, and their girls welcomed us home. Their loving, positive energy was infectious. They were ready to reveal the delegated home project. I could see that they had rearranged my living room furniture, created a playroom area, and built open shelving in the dining room. Kim described the kitchen organization efforts from Tupperware to towels. Upstairs, they had color coded the closets and replaced the wire hangers with plastic. They incorporated an additional twin sized bed into the boys' bunk room, which now hosted a place for all three brothers. Best for last was baby Hannah's room. Because my preparation for the fourth child had been to buy a pack of diapers on the way to the hospital, the team made this room extra special. They decorated it in soft pinks and grays and replaced the standard light fixture with a crystal chandelier. An upholstered glider sat next to the crib in the spot I had previously sat cross-legged on the floor to nurse Hannah. I imagined snuggling her in the warm, dark night, making amends for the sweet moments we had missed.

I could hear the children laughing in the freshly manicured backyard as they played on the tree swing that had been newly installed by the group. I sipped wine in the kitchen as Kim named all the people who had spent the entire weekend at our house in an effort to lighten our burden. I was overwhelmed by the loving gesture. They had dedicated so much of their time and energy to us. Every time I looked around the house, it reminded me that people cared. In bed that evening, I prayed that spring flooding wouldn't force us to evacuate. My recent observation of Chris had been devastating, and the potential for losing my home tipped the scale. I felt like I was drowning, but the love shown to us through the house project was like a life jacket wrapped around my body. It kept my nose above the waterline.

I was fragile at work the next morning and, evidently, wasn't hiding my stress well. A co-worker stopped by my office after our staff meeting. She asked how I was doing. I motioned for her to close the door, and I described the state of affairs. I told her about my frightening encounter with Chris, my exhaustion and fear, and the dismal possibility of spring flooding. I admitted that my burden was becoming so heavy that I was having a hard time breathing. Then, suddenly feeling embarrassed about sharing too much, I finished by saying, "I'll be fine. I just need to take one step at a time. Anyway, I scheduled an appointment with my general practitioner to get to the bottom of my breathing issues. The kids need me, so I'll make my health a top priority." My co-worker nodded her head, accepting my proposed solutions, but before she left, she reminded me that our health plan included counseling. I told her counseling had been on my to-do list. I just hadn't gotten to it yet. I was definitely interested, not only for myself but also for the children. We needed an outlet.

Glancing down at my phone, I saw that I had missed a call. I checked my voicemail. An involuntary squeak escaped from my mouth as soon as it registered. Chris had called. He left three breathy syllables, "I … love … you." I couldn't believe it. After two months of silence, he had a voice. The person I feared gone forever just minutes before seemed to be on his way back.

April 3-14, 2019 | CaringBridge journal

After recounting the events of the week, Chris said with satisfaction, "This has been a fantastic week."

I agree. It was a fantastic week. But did you catch who said it first? Chris. Yep, game changer. He has a voice.

It's amazing what just a week can bring. Seven days ago, I was visiting Chris in Lincoln with our four babes and my parents. I hadn't seen him in a week and a half, and although incredibly thin, he looked healthier. His skin tone was rosy, and he was more clicked-in. That said, as we cruised into the weekend, it seemed like he had lost steam. No doubt exhausted after a full week of therapy. And by the end of the weekend, my frustration of not being able to communicate with him was high. I left with a heavy heart, missing my best friend, even though he had been right next to me.

Thankfully, the difference from Sunday to Monday was vast. While I started my day off with an aching heart, Chris was onan upward trajectory. The good news started with his ability to tolerate the Passy-Muir valve, the part that hooks to his tracheostomy and allows him to verbalize. Because wearing it is a workout in itself, he was only been able to tolerate it for a few minutes at a time. During these stints, he would whisper one syllable per breath. "I—love—you." The first time he'd had this ability, the speech therapist asked, "Is there anything you've been wanting to say?" He looked her in the eyes and said, "Thank—you."

That's my guy.

As of last Monday, Chris has been wearing the Passy-Muir valve thirteen hours a day and expressing full, complete, and complicated sentences. In fact, the first day he wore it at length, he shared much about himself to the caregivers, saying things like, "I am a high achiever and competitive, making this a very challenging situation for me." Thank God he can participate in his care. Share what he needs when he needs it. Joke around. Talking to him on the phone for the first time in two months, I got to hear about his experience. The resounding words: "Incredibly lonely."

But it is clear he has turned the corner. Looking back, we are most definitely out of the pit and making truly incredible strides. Here are just a few on the long list of wins for the week:

- ✓ Strong head, neck, shoulder, trunk, and hip movements. New arm and leg movements. (And, just Friday, moved his elbows off the bed unassisted.)
- ✓ New scenery with his ability to drive around in a motorized wheelchair using adaptive technology, giving him control of the chair with his head movements. (The ventilator comes along with the help of therapists.)
- ✓ Strengthened eye muscles. Blinking on his own during the day and even able to hold his eyes shut for a count of fifty.
- ✓ Showering while in his wheelchair (a glorious, simple pleasure).
- ✓ Sitting on the edge of the bed with the help of his physical and occupational therapists.
- ✓ Occupational therapy working on friction-free ways to use his new arm strength.

✓ Minimal support from the ventilator. (For those who know what this means: currently only getting four breaths per minute from the ventilator, and taking 20+ breaths on his own).

✓ Stood with assistance for the first time since February 14. (Two months since he started care.)

✓ Ate his first food by mouth. Fruit smoothie and chocolate pudding.

I shouldn't be surprised by the joy of these things, after all, it's what we have been praying for. But when disaster strikes, you get into the mode of bracing yourself for the worst. I am playing around with starting to expect the best. Why shouldn't I?

I just got off the phone with Chris. He reconfirmed that this thing is measured in weeks, not days. He explained that the activities of everyday create the ebbs and flows, but at the end of the week, you can see how far you have come. He said, "Even though I am tired right now, I feel like I am on a mountaintop compared to a week ago." He went on to say, "It is attitude. It is patience. It is difficult."

Chris wrote a message on our chalk board a few months ago as a reminder to our kids. It says, "You can do hard things!" Our kids now keep telling him the same thing. "Daddy, you can do hard things." And he can. Look at him demonstrate.

By the way, on Sunday when I returned from Lincoln, I was hurting. Bad. The kind of hurt where it feels like someone is perpetually pushing down on your chest. But I would be remiss not to share the most heartwarming show of love. When we returned home that evening, our friends Kim and Matt Brakke and their girls were waiting for us. The house was glowing. Smiling faces and a glass of wine waiting for me at the entrance. This was the big reveal. Kim had orchestrated a troop of angels to work on our

house over the weekend. With the next several weeks sure
to be a challenge at home with only one free set of adult
arms, the group worked to make our home a streamlined tool.
Everything in its spot. Ship shape and more beautiful than
before. From making my baby girl's room a lovely mecca
complete \with chandelier, to creating a perfect living room
furniture arrangement, to building a new open shelving unit
in our dining room, to grooming our lawn. And so many
more things in between. I just cannot thank the group enough.
I just can't. I look around and feel so loved. Just... wow.
So beautiful on so many levels.

10

when

the shoe drops

romance is a matter of perspective

I see you

falling, we go

together but separate

the long way

Mother Mary, pray for us

teach us how to live

the stuff of dreams

reawakened

on the other side of life

the ultimate destination

home

Late April 2019

The paper on the exam table crinkled under my bottom as I tried to get comfortable. I looked in the mirror and swallowed gingerly, touching the hollow of my neck in the same place as Chris' tracheostomy. It was tender. My chest felt heavy. Phantom hands gripped my throat tighter than ever. I considered lying down. Instead, I ping-ponged through potential causes of throat, neck, and chest constriction. None were good. The GP walked into the room, shook my hand, and sat on the stool in front of the exam table, her hands on her knees.

"How are you doing?"

Forcing a smile, I explained what brought me to the clinic and summarized the series of events that made up my last few months. I told her that I thought it was in my best interest to get a full physical due to the high levels of stress in my life. I told her about the exhausting heaviness in my chest and the tightening of my throat and how for weeks they had only gotten worse. I looked at her earnestly and said, "My kids need at least one healthy parent."

The GP absorbed my words, nodding her head as she listened. She looked at me thoughtfully when I had nothing left to say. "I think we should run a few labs, but this sounds suspiciously like anxiety. And that's not to downplay your symptoms, Molly. It's common for anxiety to show up as intense chest pain or a feeling of strangulation." My fingertips absentmindedly brushed my neck, as if searching for proof of the hands that gripped so tightly. "I know it's confusing, but people report these symptoms even when they don't feel particularly anxious. Considering the extraordinary circumstances you've been dealing with, I wouldn't be surprised at all if anxiety is the cause of your heavy chest and tight throat. But let's run the tests to rule out any other possibilities."

I hadn't considered anxiety as one of the potential reasons for my physical sensations, but it was logical. "Sounds reasonable," I said.

"What's it like to be home now after such a traumatic few months?" she asked.

"Well… I feel sick that I'm not with Chris, but I know I'm where I need to be. I can finally focus on the kids," I said, rubbing my forehead. "Honestly, though, I am concerned about my boys." The weight of this statement made my heart feel like it was going to implode. My tear ducts, long dried out, stung. I closed my eyes and scrunched my nose in reaction. "The baby is happy, but the boys are distant. They bury themselves in the television and iPad, probably so they don't have to feel the pain of the last few months. But when they come out of their screen-induced comas, they are more angry and aggressive than before. Sam gets belligerent, fighting and talking back. Isaac is overly aggressive at home, but when he gets to preschool, he hides behind the door and won't take off his coat. Ben tries to keep his chin up at school, rallying friends to pray for his dad, but he cries himself to sleep at night. It's just heartbreaking."

"You're juggling a lot," she said. "You know, you may want to consider talking to someone. Counseling can be very helpful, especially when trying to navigate challenging waters."

"Actually, it's on my to-do list."

I realized how thoroughly concerned I had been that I was sick and dying. But the GP had made it clear that I was not. I felt like Mary Tyler Moore prancing around the city. *I'm going to make it after all.* I had been released from the fear of my own terminal illness, and I felt lighter after having vented some of my sorrow.

Never has anyone been as happy as me to be diagnosed with anxiety and then referred to counseling. I promptly scheduled our first sessions.

The first family counseling session would occur before Easter. Regular counseling sessions would occur on a weekly basis afterward. But first I was scheduled to spend a week with Chris in Lincoln. Barb and I had decided to switch places at the conclusion of our next visit. I would remain in Nebraska with Chris, and she would return to South Dakota with the children. I was anxious to reconnect with Chris and understand his life at Madonna. It had been two months since we had been able to talk, but it felt like years. So much had happened.

I grabbed coffee in the common area as we settled ourselves at Madonna that Saturday morning. Mesmerized by the black liquid spurting into my Styrofoam glass, I almost missed the children sneaking ice cream cups out of the kitchenette freezer. I was putting a stop to their breakfast plans when two smiling faces rounded the corner. Chris' dear friends from Omaha had come to visit. After greetings and hugs, the grandparents teamed up to entertain the children, giving us an opportunity to visit with Chris alone. Chris' face broke into a familiar smile when he saw his friends. "There they are!" he croaked jovially, working to bring them up to speed as he lie there paralyzed, skinny, pale, and with face muscles as contorted as they had been for months. I listened carefully as Chris exercised his rediscovered voice. This was the first time I'd heard him speak for any length since he had been intubated. Equally as important, it was the first time I'd heard him articulate his experience. I hung on every detail. He filled his lungs with air through the ventilator tube, and in labored, raspy stints told us his story. This was a milestone moment.

Chris' perspective was mostly what I'd expected, until he managed to say, "Yeah, this whole thing has been crazy." He rolled his eyes in an effort to gesture to his paralyzed body. "But can you believe I was arrested by the feds?" He shook his head in disbelief.

We laughed awkwardly, thinking it was a joke. But when he continued in earnest, I stopped him. "Wait. What did you say?"

He repeated, "I was arrested by the feds."

I cocked my head and squinted my eyes. "Ummm, nope, that didn't happen," I said, uncomfortably.

He looked at me confused. "Really?" A few seconds ticked by. "… Huh."

Silent panic buzzed inside my body. "You've been on a lot of drugs," I said, looking for an explanation. Chris' friends diffused the tension by saying something clever, but the comment led us to wonder if other dreams might have mingled into reality. Chris exerted himself to the point of utter exhaustion after half an hour of talking and fell asleep mid-sentence. He slept for the rest of the day. I couldn't help feeling defensive on behalf of the children. I was sorry they didn't have the opportunity to spend time with him, too.

That Sunday, we attended Easter Mass at the Madonna Chapel. Looking around during the service, I was humbled by the collective trauma of the churchgoers. Half of those in attendance were in wheelchairs. The other half were loved ones or caregivers, never far away. As I listened, the Easter message had new meaning. Jesus suffered death and was buried. He descended into hell. He rose again, taking on fuller and deeper meaning, and then ascended into heaven. The descent into hell was only half the story.

Resurrection was the other. As Father Richard Rohr would say, you can't know *up* unless you've been *down*. Hope springs anew.

Chris and I used the next week to retrace our steps. He listened to my perspective of our experience as I repeatedly dipped a swab into a glass of juice and inserted it into his mouth. He drained the sponge of its sweet liquid, appreciating the long withheld flavor as his only nourishment since February had come through a gastrointestinal tube inserted into his belly. I would stop my story after critical turning points to ask him what he had been thinking and feeling at those particular times. I watched him trying to conjure memories, which vacillated between crystal clear and hazy at best. Many of our experiences were in the same realm, but many were not. For instance, when Chris was intubated and admitted to the ICU, I felt incredible guilt. Irrational fear that he would be angry with me. Whereas, he woke up in the ICU in a Zen-like state. There was no anger. He was just grateful he could finally breathe.

Chris then exposed his bizarre, drug-induced dream world. We compared notes, chiseling dream from reality. I found that many of his dreams were grand and outrageous. Others were terrifying with him trapped in tiny spaces, alone and scared. The dreams all had something in common, though. Chris was the hero of every storyline. In one, he rescued an escaped tiger from the zoo and later halted a robbery at a convenience store and was interviewed by the news media for both. In another, he helped recovering alcoholics as part of a government sponsored therapy support group that was still in the quiet pilot phase, so not well known. These recovering alcoholics also happened to be veterans and retired biker-gang members. Chris' role had been to encourage them in their recovery and show them how to step up and get better.

I was flattered to hear that I had been chosen as the next Vera Wang model for its annual chocolate series dress in yet another dream. Chris said it was a big deal. Because of my celebrity status, we were whisked away for all kinds of glamorous activities and shortly thereafter began our own reality television show. He described in intricate detail how the cameras were installed in our home and when they were turned on and off.

Finally, I learned why Chris had been arrested by the feds. He had been participating in another government sponsored therapy program for people with traumatic injuries when he'd accidently gotten locked out of the secure facility after his mother had taken him outside to change his diaper and forgotten to prop the door open. He was caught trying to sneak back into the facility and then interrogated and arrested. Eventually, he was held for twenty four hours in solitary confinement while being tortured with music. The music ranged from show tunes, rap, and more, but the songs all had one thing in common. The lyrics were about Chris. They taunted his vulnerabilities, failures, and insecurities. And if he fought against the music, it got louder. He was forced to listen.

We had fun analyzing all of them. We determined that in his dream reality, he usually showed up as his best possible self, only to be torn down by his greatest insecurities. He was constantly attending fabulous cocktail parties with professional athletes who had some connection to both therapy and entrepreneurship programs. He was able to physically walk in these dreams, but because he had Guillain-Barré Syndrome he fell repeatedly. His unsteadiness and exhaustion disrupted and disappointed people. He was constantly ruining these parties, which caused others to question his abilities and work ethic. His fears and aspirations always pushed him forward, though.

Chris paused before one last dream reality check. "So, I'm guessing we didn't go to San Francisco?" he asked.

"Hmmm, no. Did we have fun?"

"Not really. The kids were crazy."

"Go figure," I snorted. "What did we expect?"

"I know, but we had tickets to go to a Madonna concert.
We didn't get to go because the kids were a train wreck.
They spilled all our food at the restaurant before the concert.
After that, I was just too exhausted to go."

"Why Madonna?" I squinted, failing to see the connection
to the Madonna Rehabilitation Hospital in which we were
currently sitting.

"I have no idea," he replied.

From there, our conversation naturally drifted to the children.
I described our first family counseling session and shared my
observations of how each child was handling this experience.
When Ben related the events of the last months from his perspective
to the counselor, I got goosebumps. Ben had looked at me with
exasperation and scolded, "Mom, you should have called home
more to tell us what was happening. We could have handled it."

Stunned by my nine year old's maturity, I stumbled over my
reply, "You're right, Ben. I should have shown you more respect.
I am really sorry."

"Wow." Chris' eyes were misty.

He lifted his chin and tilted his head to the left, trying to
recall something. Gazing at the ceiling, he said with consternation,
"We should talk about Hannah's legs."

"Okay, but why?" I replied, puzzled.

"She has problems with her growth plates. She has to wear braces on them." Imploring my face and seeing confusion, he followed with, "Doesn't she?"

I shook my head. "No, she's perfect." Chris looked into the distance, bewildered and relieved. "What an awful dream. Have you been worried about that the whole time?" He nodded and looked down, trying to grasp how something so real could be a dream.

Late April 2019 | continued

I observed carefully as the therapists stretched Chris' atrophied body and taught me how to assist him with isolated muscle movements. These simple movements fostered his essential building blocks for more complex and coordinated function. I took notes as the nurse aides transferred his limp body from one place to another by wrapping him in a hammock type sling connected to a device that hung from the ceiling. Once he was secured in the sling, they pushed a button and he was mechanically hoisted into the air before the aides swiveled him around and positioned him directly above his wheelchair. Then they pushed the button so he was mechanically lowered into the chair. The ease of this process was astounding after participating in the push and drag method countless times.

I watched as Chris learned to drive his electric wheelchair. He had little movement other than his neck muscles, so he controlled the chair with an attachment positioned directly next to his forehead. A single forehead bump made the wheelchair go slow. A double bump made it go fast. One therapist walked next to Chris to manage the steering. Another pulled the ventilator along as he drove, so it didn't become disconnected.

As we rolled and strolled across the hospital grounds for the first time, I felt the warm sun on my back and smelled lilacs in the air. The last time we'd been outdoors together, Chris had been a strong, vibrant man. The memory and the warm, sweet air triggered hopefulness, but our situation felt in sharp contrast and I was overcome by a wave of intense sadness and grief. I resisted the urge to grab Chris' hand and run to the car to make a fast getaway. Instead, I lagged behind as silent tears streamed down my face. There was no escaping this reality.

Chris' occupational therapist pulled me aside and handed me a folder at the end of my week in Lincoln. The folder included information on home assessments. She explained that Madonna conducts a home assessment for patients early in their stay since modifications are both time consuming and expensive. They wanted families to be prepared for the patient when it was time to return home. I wanted to be prepared too, but after review of the assessment, I knew we had a lot of work to do if Chris required a wheelchair. We had stairs at every entrance. How would he get into our house? The only bathroom we had on the first floor was a small half bath. Where would he use the bathroom? All our bedrooms were on the second floor. Where would he sleep? There were no simple solutions, and while I needed to be ready, I couldn't make any modifications yet. There were still too many unknowns.

April 15-26, 2019 | CaringBridge journal

True or false: How you do one thing is how you do everything.

This statement is the subject of a running debate we've had the last few years. It came up again while I was visiting Chris in Lincoln this week.

Observing him during therapy, I could see the determined look on his face. I saw him working, pushing, never telling the therapists he needed a break. I found my eyes wandering to the smile lines permanently etched into his face at the middle of his cheeks and the corners of his eyes. Something I really admire. I saw him appreciating the work of each nurse, therapist, aide, and physician. I saw him encouraging others. Telling the physical therapy student on her last day of rotation before going off to graduation, "You did a good job. You are ready." Sharing with one of the respiratory therapists, "Thank you so much. I really enjoy working with you." I saw him having fun with the nurses. Just this morning giving them a little dose of his karaoke favorites after they chided him to sing using his voice valve.

In the middle of an occupational therapy session, when he was trying out his budding arm movements as he moved them forward and back, diagonal and back, it struck me. How you do one thing is how you do everything. Chris has never been anything but super genuine, enthusiastic, driven, and with a laid back demeanor. A killer combination. The statement has got to be true. How you do one thing is how you do everything. Chris is tackling this experience the way he knows how. With drive, enthusiasm, authenticity, and a good natured demeanor that makes him a joy to be around. I love it.

This week, Chris' mom and I switched places. She spent the week in Fort Pierre with the kids, and I spent the week in Lincoln with Chris. It was a really important week for me. After two months, Chris and I were finally together. No immediate threat invading our space, no constant beeping, or screaming medical alarms. He has a voice. We were able to catch up on the last several weeks, sort out the dreams from the reality, and talk about our incredible children, incredible family, incredible friends and community. I was able to participate in his therapy sessions, participate in this new chapter of our lives. We took a walk outside with a wheelchair, two therapists, and a ventilator. It smelled like lilacs. We had movie night. We were able to consciously be partners in life again. Heaven.

Chris is more alert and has growing endurance. His core is getting stronger, and this week he was able to support his trunk with no assistance while sitting on the side of his bed with help from the therapists. His arms are starting to come to life, and he was able to work with the same motions he would use to control a joystick. His legs are regaining movement, and he did minimal assist squats on a special table raised to eight degrees with a sliding backrest. His voice is getting stronger, and he resumed ventilator weaning after a weeklong break. He is returning to some normal activity, and he has graduated to three meals a day, albeit soft and pureed ones. The double vision, completely frozen eyelids, and minimal head and shoulder movements are but a distant memory. I feel like the clouds are parting.

After being cheered on by one of the therapists, Chris said, "Thank you for your enthusiasm. Enthusiasm matters. It really does." Hmmm, good one.

Once again, how you do one thing is how you do everything.

It has to be a true statement.

11

when

the shoe drops

romance is a matter of perspective

I see you

falling, we go

together but separate

the long way

Mother Mary, pray for us

teach us how to live

the stuff of dreams

reawakened

on the other side of life

the ultimate destination

home

Early May 2019

I was becoming a regular. Each week, I would enter through the double doors and glance at the pictures hanging on the walls as I walked down the hallway. I would slip inside the door on the right, nod at the woman behind the desk, and then wait my turn to sit in my usual seat and unload. In a quiet room just for me. No distractions. No responsibilities except to explore my innermost thoughts and feelings, drain the toxic energy, and get perspective.

Counseling was my pressure release. I see it as a sign of strength to dive into the deep and examine thoughts and behaviors with someone trained to listen. Especially given an emotional disturbance to sort through. And, let's face it, emotional disturbances are the inevitable waves that crash onto life's shore. I can't stop the wave no matter how hard I might try. So, I might as well learn to surf. Develop resilience. Because emotions control thoughts, and thoughts control behaviors, I am well served to learn how to ride the wave rather than get sucked into the undertow. My counseling sessions were my surfing lessons.

I let it all out. How I felt possessive of my roles as wife and mother. I knew I needed to be with my children at home, and Barb's willingness to take ownership of Chris' daily care was the gift that allowed me to do that. I couldn't duplicate myself, and I was lucky enough to have someone else who loved Chris with all her heart to help. Barb never once made me feel guilty. She was clear that staying in Lincoln didn't inconvenience her in any way. Having been widowed and retired for more than ten years, she had structured her life with a flexibility that allowed her to be available to her children and grandchildren at a moment's notice.

But as I backed up to care for my children and give Barb space to care for hers, I unwittingly forfeited my primary role in Chris' recovery. It was no longer Chris and Molly. It was now Chris and Barb… and Molly. I heard about the events of Chris' day *through Barb*. I learned of his recovery progress *through Barb*. I heard about setbacks *through Barb*.

I was hungry for the things that recognized my role as the wife. Family meetings with Chris' care team for my benefit. Physical therapy goals that involved me. My name and number on Chris' dry erase board. Basically, any reminder of my importance in his life. Any reminder that I was married to a man, not the patient who I felt had been reduced to an infantile state under his mother's care. She would touch his shoulder, move in toward his face, and share encouraging words of support or describe the next steps in his care with a cooing voice and smile. He would mirror her facial movements by smiling and nodding in response. One day, I walked into Chris' hospital room and heard the music that Barb had left playing in the background. It was a lullaby. I did my best to act like I didn't notice, but it made me furious.

Okay, everything made me furious.

Anger is my default emotion in stress. I wasn't furious because I had a fraught relationship with my mother-in-law. I was furious because my husband *was* an infant. I was angry because the boundaries of my life had been severely violated. It was nobody's fault. Barb wasn't doing anything to hurt me. She was his mother. Chris *was*, for all intents and purposes, an infant, unable to care for himself. I just felt alone and gutted. I mourned the loss of us. The "us" I'd known before Chris' illness. The "us" that understood one another deeply.

My counselor listened, helping me break down my situation and myself. The good, the bad, and the ugly. How I didn't want my loved ones to be overloaded with the ugliest parts of my burden.

How I was mourning the life we had been living before Chris'
sudden illness. How the trauma of the last several months continued
to echo in my mind, causing me to jolt from the nightmare even
though I was already awake. The first few months in the hospital
had been about survival. Life and death. I hadn't had the time
or ability to untangle the knot of emotions that formed. Now,
as they unraveled, I had to deal with their after-effect as I coped
with continual change and adjustment while supporting my
children through the same. It was a delicate balance. It required
patience with myself and everyone around me.

I thought about Barb. How gut wrenching must it be to see
your adult child in Chris' position? Barb had a life that allowed her
to be there, but what else was she giving up? She slept on a pull-out
couch in Chris' hospital room, her things shoved into a backpack
in the corner. At night, she would prepare for bed by taping Chris'
eyes closed, and then, because his voice valve was removed from
his tracheostomy when he slept, she would listen for him to click
his tongue when he needed something. On top of that, she was the
eyes and ears for his spouse. And here I was, the spouse, on edge,
raw with emotion and quick to anger, not connecting how Barb
made it easy for me to sleep in my own bed, sandwiched between
the cherub faces of my little boys, thanking God I was safely
at home. Yet the anger still welled.

Adding to my conflicting emotions, I was overwhelmed with
gratitude for the continuing boosts of love from family, friends,
and community. On this marathon, their many kindnesses were
like perfectly timed water stops along the way. Refreshing. Energy-
giving. I was humbled by the many people conspiring for our good,
supporting us in so many ways and with gifts that hadn't even
been revealed to me yet. I would talk about these many beautiful
shows of support during my counseling sessions. It was clear that

collectively they were the wind nudging me along, making my journey easier. Then the anger faded again, replaced by gratitude.

But the anger never disappeared, nor did any of my emotions. In fact, my many emotions competed for my attention, just like the children, Chris, work, and life in general. Every emotion wanted out at the same time, but I pretended not to hear any of them unless in counseling. Detachment became an effective coping method. But when I got a chink in my armor from the daily combat of life, my emotions found an opening, and the first one through was always anger. Not only was anger efficient, it was effective. It shut everything else down. It gave me a shield and the quick fuel necessary to do the next thing on my list. Anger kept the more vulnerable rooms of my compartmentalized life locked. It sealed me off from the sadness that I feared would be crippling if allowed out. Anger flared if I felt the need to be protective of my children. Or when I was overtired. Or overwhelmed. Or frustrated.

As time went by, my practice of detachment and routine anger began to make my other emotions difficult to access. Only when my counselor held space for me to talk freely would my other feelings creep out of hiding. Nevertheless, sadness always made me feel like I was falling. Counseling created greater equilibrium, which allowed me to lower my shield of anger and process my feelings so I could better understand why I reacted in certain ways and at certain times. This vulnerability restored balance and with balance came better, more reasoned thinking. Counseling gave me the insight I needed to make intentional adjustments to my directional rudder. It was a phenomenal opportunity for growth.

April 27–May 14, 2019 | CaringBridge journal

Have you ever watched water boil? I have. I've watched water boil. And, I don't know about you, but if I hadn't already seen it happen time and time again, I might question whether water actually boils when heated. While watching and waiting, I might think, *I've heard this works, but I am not sure it's actually going to. Shouldn't it have happened by now?*

Watching water boil is one of those things that makes you more impatient by the moment. You see the water, still and calm. You feel the heat radiating from the stovetop. You look at the clock. Fingers drumming. You double check to make sure the burner is set to high. You look at the clock again. Time stands still. You look into the pot. Nothin'. Oh wait, is that a bubble? You scrutinize. Nope, not yet. Still waiting. Deep breath. Why does it take so long? And then, all of a sudden, when you have resigned yourself to forever, the water starts rolling. It's go time.

And that, my friends, is the recovery from Guillain-Barré Syndrome in a nutshell. It's just when you think nothing is happening that you realize a lot is happening. I look back and reflect on six weeks ago when Chris was not blinking, breathing, eating, talking, literally moving a muscle without assistance. Pretty much nothing. The pot was still. Fast forward to today, Chris is starting to sizzle, and bubbles are rolling to the surface.

When people ask me how Chris is doing, I reply honestly, "Really well." Every time I see him, I see signs that things are improving. His blink is increasingly more instinctual. His voice is stronger, and he sounds more like himself. He sang *Happy Birthday* to Isaac on his fourth birthday last week.

Chris' swallow is stronger, and he just got clearance to drink regular liquids. The thrill of getting to drink out of a glass for the first time as opposed to a swab or spoon was surprising. Of all the things that make a person feel normal, evidently drinking from a glass is right up there. Chris graduated to solid foods as well. Last Friday the boys and I had the pleasure of watching him eat a trial Level Four meal. Turkey wrap, Asian cabbage salad, apples, and carrots. He loved it.

While Chris can't move his hands or feet yet, he has muscle activation in many of the muscles down to his ankles and wrists. The kids and I got to play a form of table hockey with him last week with the help of the therapists. Then, while Chris stood with a stand assist machine for sixteen minutes, the therapist had him pushing a ball to the kids. The kids would catch the ball and throw it back. How fun for the boys after all these months. They danced around in celebration, and Samuel turned "the Dab" into a symbol of encouragement. We are so appreciative of the physical and occupational therapists at Madonna for incorporating our whole family into Chris' care and rehabilitation.

Here's an excellent example of our diverse landscape. Early last week Chris woke up feeling low. His ventilator weaning hadn't worked the previous night. Buzzers and bells rang every time the ventilator support was ratcheted back. He felt like he was making very little progress. *Would he be on a ventilator forever?* He could never have guessed that by noon the next day he would be breathing room air. The beauty of Madonna's respiratory therapists, with approval from their pulmonary team, is that they are willing to be creative. The team regrouped and said that since Guillain-Barré is different, we are going to try something different too. So, rather than put him on room air at night and full ventilator support during the day, which is what they do for most patients, they flip-flopped the equation. They put him on room air during the day with full ventilator support at night. It worked like a charm. Chris has been off the ventilator during his waking hours since early last week. Now, that is a milestone. "How do you feel?" I asked.

He smiled. "I feel normal, like a real human. It feels great. Natural."

I am thankful that Chris was able to FaceTime into the kids' music concerts a few weeks ago. Thankful that Chris could watch Ben accept the Volunteer of the Year award on his behalf from the Pierre Youth Orchestra. We were so proud when Ben set his cello down, confidently walked to the microphone and, with head tilted upward and on tippy toes, told the audience, "Thanks for praying!" I am thankful for the continuing gifts and support of all kinds. For the teachers who have lifted our kids up during this difficult time. For the meal train that has simplified the logistics of feeding the children so I can instead focus on the children themselves. The audio memory montage recorded and sent to Chris. The surprise photo session of the kids that was coordinated unbeknownst to me and the resulting portraits hung and waiting for me on Mother's Day. The countless hours spent in preparation for the upcoming benefit event being organized by our friends. Seriously, people. We are being carried, just carried.

In the spirit of Mother's Day, I want to recognize Chris' mom, Barb Maxwell, who shows her love and devotion. Every. Single. Day. She is a bright light for us and to everyone who has crossed her path, I know. Watching her in action, it's no surprise Chris is so incredible. I also want to recognize my mom, Judy Weisgram, who is always right behind me, sometimes propping me up and other times saluting me. She chooses enthusiasm, positivity, creativity, love, and strength each day... and it shows.

I want to be like the two of you when I grow up.

It's been nearly a week, and I am still laughing.

Picture this. Chris is in the gym on the long-term acute rehab unit. He is lying on an elevated queen sized mat where his therapist has him in a full body stretch. At the conclusion of the session, the therapist does a series of maneuvers to get him back into his electric wheelchair. She slides him over to the edge, rolls him onto his side, hoists him to a sitting position, crosses his hands on his lap, and, in a rocking "one-two-three," pivots and shimmies him from the mat to the chair. A thing of beauty. In the process of this transition, one of Chris' arms gets loose and flops around on the bed next to him, willy-nilly as he tries to control it with the little arm strength he has available. Chris says, "Sheesh, Weekend at Bernie's over here." If you know this movie reference, congratulations, you are age forty or older. Chris nailed it. All of us around the mat promptly got a case of the church giggles. It felt wrong but, oh, so right.

I am not saying paralysis is a picnic. In fact, the extreme vulnerability Chris has experienced is nearly unimaginable. Not comfortable, very humbling. Definitely no picnic. That said, I have recently asked myself, "Should we be having this much fun?" That sounds odd, I know, but truth be told, we have been having so much fun together.

It might be Chris' amazing attitude and great sense of humor. Maybe it's because we have missed each other so much and appreciate the ability to talk to one another. Perhaps it's because our parents, family, friends, neighbors, and co-workers have found numerous ways to ease our burden. Or maybe it's due to the upward trajectory of Chris' health, having just recently graduated from both speech and respiratory therapy. Likely, it's a combination of all of them. It's always a combination, isn't it?

In regard to Chris' health, I am happy to report that, as of yesterday, Chris proclaimed himself to be "tube-free in room 233!" Nothing artificial is connected to him any longer. Goodbye, gastrointestinal tube. Goodbye, tracheostomy and oximeter. Fare thee well, ventilator. Do good for your next patient.

A scene from the beginning flashes through my mind. I am sitting in the ICU next to Chris' hospital bed. It's four o'clock in the morning. He is sleeping, but I am on high alert. His pain, temperature fluctuations, and inability to speak are making me jumpy. I remember the noises, Darth Vader breathing sounds and constant beeping. I remember feeling sick and lost. In that moment, a wave of hatred for all of it crossed my mind and body. *How did this happen?* It came out of nowhere. Anger at the ventilator. Anger at the beeping machines. I resented all of it. Until it struck me. My perspective was backward. Instead of hatred for those machines and their dreaded sounds, I should feel love. Those sounds were music to my ears, whether I totally felt it or not, because they were part of the things that were keeping my partner alive. I should appreciate them and send prayers of thanks for those ingenious people who spent their days devising these lifesaving technologies.

It is not lost on me that if this had happened thirty years ago, Chris would have died on February 19. Instead, because of the ventilator, medical professionals, and all the other things working in unison, he didn't. He is alive. Chris has a second chance. We have a second chance. What do you do with a second chance? That is a big question.

Well, one thing you could do is have a party, I guess. And on May 24 we did just that. We celebrated Hannah, our beautiful baby girl, as she turned one year old. We went birthday bowling, Madonna style. The therapists turned Chris' therapy session into a festive party in the hospital hallway. With Chris in his electric wheelchair, each child had a turn to sit on their dad's lap. In front of them, the therapists had set up a sloping track pointed toward bowling pins. We placed Chris' hands on a rubber bowling ball positioned on the track, and together father and child pushed the ball with all their might. Chris' arms would burst forth and then dangle at his sides after the launch. The ball rolled down the slope, gaining momentum until it hit the pins. We cheered and hollered obnoxiously with the full approval of everyone. Madonna probably hasn't heard that kind of ruckus in a while.

Before each roll, Isaac would ceremoniously place metallic birthday hats on every pin. Then as the other children had their turn to sit on Daddy's lap, he would have my dad hold him upside down by his feet so he could be the backdrop to the makeshift lane. It was perfect. Chris said, "Well, they almost ripped my arms off, but I wouldn't have it any other way."

Hannah ate bits of pizza and dug around in Grandma Barb's homemade chocolate cake that was decorated with a single pacifier on top. I was secretly hoping she would dive in face first to rescue her passy, but instead she snatched it with her hand, popped it into her mouth, and squished the cake between her fingers, making chocolate cake sandcastles. Light in her eyes, she smiled her big, beautiful smile. Happy birthday, baby. We are so lucky you are ours.

Chris continues to make this easy for us. He leads us from that hospital bed. He chooses ease and perspective, so we choose ease and perspective. Even without the use of his body, he steadies us. Not letting us fall. Thank you, Chris. Honestly, if I had to do it all over, I'd pick you again. I don't just love you (and I do), but I also really, really like you.

12

when

the shoe drops

romance is a matter of perspective

I see you

falling, we go

together but separate

the long way

Mother Mary, pray for us

teach us how to live

the stuff of dreams

reawakened

on the other side of life

the ultimate destination

home

Early June 2019

The month began with Chris officially ready for rehab
after ten weeks at LTAC and fifteen weeks on the ventilator.
He transferred to Madonna's Acute Rehabilitation floor ready
to work. Before they let him go, though, his care team at
LTAC awarded him the Madonna Spirit Award, recognizing
his positivity and determination. They encouraged him to keep
up the good work. It was a surprisingly bittersweet moment.

A few weeks before his transfer, Chris had begun to affectionately
refer to his hospital room as the "tree house" because the tree
directly outside of his second floor window had leafed out, making
his primary view lush, green foliage. It was calming to be in his
room when the window was open and listen to the leaves rustle
audibly in the breeze. LTAC had become our safe place. The place
where Chris was getting better. The place where Chris had
developed deep trust in the nurses and caregivers. Friendly faces
came in and out of his room on a regular basis. These amazing
medical professionals had transformed the space from a hospital
room into a healing room. But, while it had become comfortable,
it was time to leave the nest.

"Who would have thought we'd ever be sad to leave
Long-Term Acute Care?" I joked.

Chris shook his head and said, "Seriously."

Madonna's Acute Rehab, located on the first floor of the facility,
is technically a different hospital than LTAC. But the major
difference is the pace. Because people aren't tethered to ventilators,
they don't spend entire days in their rooms. They still need plenty
of assistance, but independence is the goal. Chris had developed
enough strength and mobility to drive his electric wheelchair with

a joystick controlled by his arm. I would set his floppy hand on an attachment shaped like a goalpost, and he would use his shoulder strength to heave his arm forward and backward to operate the chair. Chris liked the freedom of *go*, often rolling a little faster in his big electric wheelchair than I could walk. And because patients were rolling to and from the gym on a regular basis, Chris quickly made new friends. I watched as he resumed looking at people until they returned his smile. These connections provided him the life giving energy that he so craved.

May 31-June 12, 2019 | Caring Bridge journal

The other day Chris was doing therapy on the acute rehabilitation floor at Madonna, or "big boy rehab" as I've dubbed it. The acute rehab gym at Madonna is hoppin'. There are a lot of people working it, and the energy is palpable.

A large sound suddenly came from the corner. With a jump, everyone collectively turned in that direction. The source of the noise was a man surrounded by two therapists. "Is he crying?" I said in quiet horror.

Chris said, "No, I think he is laughing."

Oh, this guy wasn't just laughing. He was bellowing. The kind of laughter that causes tears to stream down your face until it turns into strange, happy sobs. The hushed, heavy din of the gym suddenly lightened, and you could feel everyone take in the healing magic induced by laughter. How cool is that? Our bodies are designed to laugh.

At least two important things happened on the rehab front this week. First, Chris was transferred to the acute rehabilitation floor. They tell us that this is where things really start to happen.

At this level of therapy, not only will Chris have access to some technologically advanced machines, but he will also get to start therapy sessions in the pool, something he is excited about. Second, starting last week, we began witnessing slight movements in Chris' fingers. This is extremely exciting, as the distal areas of the body are the most uncertain to return from a recovery standpoint. This gives us hope that he will regain the use of his hands.

Chris keeps joking that he is in a race with our baby Hannah to meet developmental milestones. She may win at using her hands and taking her first step, but with flippant pride he said, "At least I got her on potty training."

There is a big shindig coming up this Friday. It's the Support Chris Maxwell event at Drifters that our amazing friends have come together to organize. I am kind of nervous. All eyes on us. But I am excited, too. These are our people. People I admire and respect, all coming together to support Chris. Give him "the Dab" of encouragement. It's going to be such fun. A real celebration. We are coming together to celebrate Chris' rebirth. A time when we thankfully get to talk about him in the present and future tense rather than the past. For entertainment, we are so lucky to have our incredibly talented pianist friend, Matthew Mayer, come all the way from Omaha to share his gift of music. If you haven't heard him play, you just have to come out.

At the event, there will be a slide show of Chris' unreal (all too real) experience. He gave us permission to use these pictures, even though, understandably, they are not how anyone would want to be seen. He said he is totally comfortable sharing them. They are just the truth of this experience.

Jess Rasmussen gave me a preview of the slideshow. It was fantastically surreal to see our journey captured neatly to music. I looked over to see that Ben was watching it too, and boy oh boy was he wearing some big emotions for a nine year old. With shock in his voice, he said, "It's so... sad." I could feel the draw of the ocean before the release of his emotional wave. Tears rolled as the feelings crashed to the surface. Through his sobs, he said, "Mom, these are both happy and sad tears. I just miss Dad. I need him." I know, honey, I know. Me too.

When the kids and I returned home on Sunday night, there was a bunch of activity. Cars lined the road to our home, and friends met us in the driveway. *What the heck is going on here?* As they guided us to the backyard, the kids broke into a full-fledged sprint paired with squeals of delight when they saw the big, bad Rainbow Playset installed in our backyard. Guys, this thing is fab. An absolute kid magnet. I saw a whole bunch of people as I rounded the corner. Rotarians.

Chris loves the Rotarians. He always refers to them as a bunch of people who want to do Good in the world. As I understand it, after my sweet friends seeded the idea, the Rotarians ran with it in a huge way. I can't tell you how overwhelmingly touched I am. Just a whole bunch of people doing Good in the world. This playset will always be a symbol of love.

The words thank you feel less and less sufficient. They are small compared to what we feel. That said, thank you is what we have right now. So, *thank you.* Please know it comes from a place of deep sincerity.

Here is Chris' response to everyone's generosity and kindness. "I just hope I can do enough Good in the world to give it all back." He is totally a Rotarian.

Please forgive me, but I have this song stuck in my head. Probably only a select few of you will appreciate it. Those with elementary school age kids surely will. It's from the Lego Movie 2. The song is called Everything's Not Awesome. This song pretty well sums it up, I think. Life isn't always going to be the idealistic (perhaps flat) form of awesome. In my experience, though, it's true... when we stick together, everything is better. Our family, friends, and community have all come together in the most amazing ways, locking together like Lego pieces to build beautiful and intricate experiences that have made a lasting impression on our hearts.

Hope to see you at seven o'clock this Friday night at Drifters in Fort Pierre. Music, drinks, and Good people. We are having a party, and the only thing missing will be Chris although, rumor has it, he may make a FaceTime appearance.

Mid-June 2019

Major changes were taking place inside me. I examined them with my counselor. The roles I used to play as wife and mother, and the way I typically acted, were ill suited to the current reality. The changing dynamic that resulted from this illness had required me to reawaken parts of my personality as well as reconsider my identity within my partnership with Chris.

Chris thrives on relationships. They fill him. He knows everyone to some degree because he values community, and he isn't just friendly. He genuinely wants to know people. He has no hesitation reaching out his hand for a quick introduction. I am different and needed to be after Chris and I married. If I didn't keep to a schedule, we might never leave or get anywhere. Case in point: a restaurant. Before leaving a restaurant, Chris would look around to see who he could visit with because the reality of a small town is that you know many of the people you see out on any given night. By the time we would have stopped at the tables of all the people we knew, other people would have arrived, and we would have to make the rounds again. It's not that I don't enjoy people. I do. Very much. But I prefer a heart to heart conversation with a few, rather than short visits with many. To conserve my energy, I gave Chris the social liaison role in our marriage and retreated to the background. I had retreated so much that I hardly viewed myself as a social person anymore.

After Chris' illness, I became the spokesperson for the family. I stepped out of my self-imposed retreat. I shared our story on CaringBridge and communicated directly with friends and family of mine, ours, and Chris' when I was able. This resulted in numerous conversations about things I was learning and how those truths related to them and everyone in some meaningful way. It was beautiful to discover that Chris had the most wonderful friends. I had conversations with individuals I had previously only known by name. Now, I understood Chris' enthusiasm for his relationships. I was dazzled by these people. It made me appreciate him more and rethink my stance on energy conservation. But it made me miss Chris even more, too.

June 12-16, 2019 | CaringBridge journal

Anyone who has driven by our house in the last few years has likely seen my dad mowing the lawn or picking weeds. We have never once asked him to do this. He just does it. He is an acts of service kind of guy. In this case, Love is a nicely manicured lawn.

Since Chris got sick, those driving by have also probably seen my dad's white pickup truck parked in front of our house early in the morning and late at night. In the morning, my dad shows up to help with the flurry of activity in getting kids ready for school and daycare. He comes complete with the sack lunches he made for the boys in advance. He loads the kids into his truck and takes them to their respective places, while I take a deep breath, fill my coffee mug, and move on to work. Throughout the day, he is thinking through what the kids and I are going to eat for dinner and may even slide a gallon of milk into my fridge if he sees we are running low.

At night, he and my mom help run the boys to baseball when it is clear I can't divide myself or a late night wouldn't be good for the little ones. Then Dad launders the boys, giving baths and telling stories. I find myself slowing down to listen when he tells the stories from when he was a little boy. I revert back to my younger self, and ask, "What happened next?" and "Did that really happen, Dad?" I love those stories.

We've had a special tradition every Sunday after church since I can remember. My dad makes dinner for the whole family, including my 99-year-old Nana. My mom is most definitely the co-chef with her lovely salads and garnishes, but my dad takes ownership of the meat and potatoes. It is a delicious dinner. We lovingly refer to it as "a Dad meal." There is always a pretty presentation with wine before dinner and coffee served with the dessert my Nana brings along. I love Sundays. I really do. Sunday dinners are one of my favorite parts of moving back to my hometown. They are sacred.

Before he got sick, Chris always did the dishes after dinner on Sundays. He did it so consistently that it became the role he assumed. We just assumed he would do it. We have missed Chris on Sundays and every day, not just because we have to do the dishes, but because we have an empty chair at the table that can't be filled by anyone else.

Both my dad and Chris are the type of people who leave a place better than when they found it. In more ways than one.

Chris' event Friday night at Drifters was spectacular, by the way. I gave and received so many hugs. I watched as my friends hustled and bustled at the event they worked so hard to produce. Everyone came together so beautifully. Friend Carrie Mikkonen was able to articulate my feelings when she said, "This is the hardest part and the best part. Feel the love."

It's hard to be in a place of receiving. It really is. But it is amazing, too. I kept looking around and thinking, *Wow, people are here because they care about us and want us to be okay.* Everything about the night, the place where the event was hosted, the music we were listening to, the friends and family gathered from near and far, the donations of auction items and those who purchased them, the swiftness in my friends' steps as they kept everything flowing and on schedule, was for us.

We were able to connect with Chris live through FaceTime. He looked great. He spoke with a bubbling yet humble eloquence that was so him. After the event, Isaac said, "My favwit powt was when Dad towlked to us. It was a ce-wa-bway-shion." It truly was a celebration. Mission accomplished, my friends. We feel the love.

Happy Father's Day, Chris. You are exactly who I want you to be. You are showing all of us what patience, persistence, and a positive attitude look like. You are teaching our kids resilience through your example. Your perfection comes in imperfect ways and at imperfect times, but it comes. I am seeing so much beauty in the kiln. Keep smiling. You are a wonderful husband and dad. We love you more than you will ever know.

And Happy Father's Day to my Dad, too. I will never forget how you and mom showed up during this time in our lives. You are taking care of me, tending to my bruises, and letting me know everything will be all right. I love you.

July 2019

Madonna had become home away from home for Chris. A place of love and safety as he continued to make slow motion progress. I looked forward to going "home" to Chris. The long drives were therapeutic, and the time I spent with him was satisfying. The children loved going too, reconnecting with their dad and enjoying the Lincoln Children's Museum, the zoo, and (of course) the hotel pool. In fact, they begged to move there. Sam even watched the housing market, pointing out houses he would like to live in.

Barb had secured on-campus housing at Madonna by this point. Her living arrangement was basically a hotel room with a kitchenette. When she offered to have the children come to Lincoln one at a time to spend a week during the summer, I instinctually pulled them closer to me. I didn't want my family to be broken apart any further, and I fought the ugly urge to protect my role as mother and not "forfeit" this role to Barb, too. *Patience*, I counseled myself. Eventually, I agreed to let them go. During their special weeks in Lincoln, the children rode on Chris' lap as he drove his wheelchair down the halls. They pushed the button that mechanically lowered him into the pool for water therapy. They stretched his legs. They fed him. Barb read books to them as they waited until therapy was over. Then, at the end of the day, they crawled into the hospital bed with Chris, snuggling and watching movies. The time spent was healing for everyone.

I have a great idea for a Peanut M&M's commercial. Seriously, this is good. Just the right combination of tear jerker and heart warmer.

The first shot shows a sweet baby girl with blond hair and blue eyes looking upon her dad who is hospital bound and sitting in his wheelchair. It's clear the burgeoning toddler doesn't know him well by the tentative expression she wears each time the mom brings her near him. The dad has an understanding yet agonized look on his face. The viewer can tell he is coaching himself in patience. All he wants to do is cuddle her, put her soft cheek next to his.

The second shot is of a dim but warmly lit hospital room. The mom scoots the dad to one side of the twin hospital bed so that there is enough room for her to slide in next to him. She brings the baby with her, making a nest between them. The baby girl stiffens and shimmies away from the dad. That is, until the mom hands her a cup of Peanut M&M's and says, "Daddy is so hungry. Please feed him!"

The little girl thinks about it and finally grabs an M&M from the cup, gingerly bringing her hand to his mouth before snatching it away somewhat fearfully. She tries again and again until finally she, while not interested in them personally, dispenses the M&M's liberally into the dad's mouth.

The dad's face lights up as he joyfully exclaims, "Mmmmmm! Thank you!" Each time he says this, the baby gets a pleased look on her face and agrees with her own soft "Mmmm" sound, her head shaking up and down. Then she gives him another and another. After some time, he looks up at the mom who is gazing

upon the scene, and says, "My heart is exploding."
They look at each other and smile. The same smile they
shared the day she was born.

The M&M logo flashes across the screen and the text reads,
"Bringing people together since 1941."

This is how we spent Friday night in real life. While my parents
took the boys swimming at the hotel pool, I brought Hannah
to Chris' hospital room. Though Hannah had not completely
stiff armed him, she had been giving Chris the I-will-only-
smile-at-you-if you-are-at-a-distance kind of vibe. But the
Peanut M&M's changed the game.

The activity was an icebreaker. In addition to feeding Chris
a monster's serving of M&M's, by the end of the night, Hannah
had warmed up so thoroughly that she was patting him on
the head and even leaning into his chest head first, her version
of a hug. Not only did Chris look at me and say, "My heart
is exploding," but he also said, "Oh, man, I am going to get
a stomachache, but I can't stop her. This is too good."

When the kids and I first saw Chris last Thursday morning,
he greeted us with hugs. Hugs! He lifted his arms and wrapped
them around us. Sweet Jesus, what a warm welcome. We got
to Lincoln just in time to participate in the weekly Madonna
therapy outing. Bowling, baby! Parkway Lanes beware.
Maxwell boys in da house. Bowling balls shot like cannons
in more directions than just the pins. Amid fist pumping and
muscle flexing, the crew walked like Egyptians to more than one
'80s and '90s-era tune. And even though he was not the only
Maxwell boy to use the ball slope, the disability accommodation
for bowling, Chris somehow still got the high score. Typical.

We celebrated with some good bar food that Chris fed himself using a Velcro cuff strapped to his hand that kept the fork in place. By the end of the meal, he ditched the fork and ate the french fries with his fingers. Take that, GBS.

During therapy sessions we kept the hospital entertained. More accurately, Isaac kept 'em entertained. Giggling people would approach us and report what the munchkin had said. One time it was, "Oh my, your son just walked by the salon where a bunch of 80-year-old women were getting their hair done. He gave them a nonchalant wave and with a wink and twinkle confidently said, 'Hi girls.' Before sauntering off, he looked the other direction and hollered to someone, 'I've got this.'" Oh yeah, did I mention he was fully suited up in his blue Power Ranger costume? So stinkin' cute.

Chris keeps getting stronger and more functional each week. It's incredible, really. He has new-found trunk strength and the ability to lift his arm high enough to place his hand on the wheelchair joystick, giving him the ability to move whenever and wherever he darn well pleases. He can scratch his own nose and even brush his teeth with an assisted cuff that holds the toothbrush in place. He has increasing movement and strength in his hands, fingers, and wrists. He also officially has movement in his feet. It's slow but sure. It's almost like he has been frozen in ice, Han Solo style, and each week thaws out a little more.

These are big things. Each another step toward independence. He is on a good trajectory. Signs of greater things to come. Hallelujah. The irony of it all is that these things, things that have taken agonizing time, patience, and determination to achieve, seem like the most natural things in the world once they are back.

The marquee at the hospital entrance says, "Every day is Independence Day at Madonna!" In the wake of the recent Fourth of July holiday, it seems fitting to say that freedom is a wonderful thing. The most natural thing in the world. That said, we need to remember not to take it for granted. Every step toward independence, and each step beyond, calls for appreciation. We are thankful.

August 14, 2019

Therapy was working, as was Chris' attitude. Muscle activation, strength, and mobility were returning to his body, and the visions and goals he once had for his life were returning to his mind. He was not yet in control of his landscape, but he sat firmly in the driver's seat, considering the maneuvers available to him. He was being strategic. I was impressed.

"I am like a start-up company," Chris said as he nodded to a picture hanging on the wall. The picture he reference displayed an original quote, something he had said through letter board communication when he was in the ICU. A friend had printed the quote on canvas and sent it to him as a reminder. It read:

Success starts with patience, persistence, positivity, proactive action, passion, purpose, planning, process, and knowing that your perfection will come in imperfect ways and at imperfect times.

"This is the philosophy I use for all my clients at work. But it's proving to be applicable in this situation, too."

"How so?"

"I believe everyone needs a *purpose*, a big vision. And this purpose is spurred by *passion*, the fuel necessary to go forward. In my case, the purpose is to return home ambulatory."

I nodded.

"Once you've defined your purpose, you have to pursue it even when you are fearful. Look at me. It's possible that I might not achieve my purpose, but I still need to try. If I want certainty, I could give up. But then I would most certainly be disappointed."

Motioning to the picture again with his head, he referenced the words *plan* and *process*. "My therapists and I have developed a *plan* for my recovery. We're following a set of *processes* that build upon my current functionality and push me to the next level. But that's not the special ingredient. I believe a big vision needs *positivity*, aka sunlight, and *proactive action*, aka water, to grow. Being paralyzed and ripped from my life is not easy. But I cannot feed the 'not easy' part. I have to surround myself in positivity if I want to achieve my purpose. And I don't really mean surround myself in positivity. I mean *be* positivity. There is always going to be negativity around us, but we get to choose how we enter every situation. We can choose to be a positive, proactive force in the world. Or we can choose the opposite. This *perspective* helps me find ways to be proactive, for instance, taking extra protein, fish oils, and weekend workouts. And I would much rather be motivated by positive momentum than fear. It's a nuance, but it's a much better energy."

"I like where you are going with this, Chris," I said with admiration.

"And then it's like a dance," he continued. "The effort takes *patience* and *persistence* simultaneously. You have to know when to push and when to let up. I can push my body to the brink, but then I need to take a break. If I keep pushing at the wrong times, my effort becomes counterproductive.

"I believed this before, but I *know* it now," he reflected. "*Perfection is imperfect*. It's not always easy, but if I take the perspective that 'this is all for me' and 'I am exactly where I am supposed to be,' then I am present to everything available to me in this moment. Whether or not I accomplish the purpose I originally set out to achieve, I will have followed the illuminated path, rather than hesitating at the beginning, never braving the journey."

July 15-August 19, 2019 | CaringBridge journal

I have found myself thinking a lot about cause and effect lately. I am a strong believer in the idea that what you do today shows up tomorrow. I know the concept is basic understanding. Table talk, really. Nevertheless, I am astounded by how true it is. What I am today is a product of my choices in the proverbial yesterday. What I am tomorrow is a product of my choices today.

As I write this, I am watching Chris reverse his wheelchair into a weight machine designed to work the triceps, shoulders, and back. It's Saturday. We are in the Madonna gym outside of scheduled therapy hours alone, which is probably for the best since we are jamming to tunes. A little too loud. For context, Chris woke up this morning and immediately requested ice packs for his hips and knees. He is sore and rightly so. He worked hard this week.

Chris knows he has choices. And what I've learned through conversations with him is that when the therapists give him options for what he would like to work on, most of the time, he chooses the hardest thing. He knows his investment of time and effort now will allow him to reap the benefits he is looking to achieve later. So, because Chris wants additional strength, he puts in the effort today so that the strength is available tomorrow. He has proven this true, week after week. The effects of his therapies and efforts appear in the days following.

Choosing to go to the gym on a Saturday after a long week of therapy, and with an aching body as well as hands and feet that are on Guillain-Barré fire, is admirable. But what I respect most is that when Chris can't physically do something, he doesn't sigh and say, "I can't do that anymore." Instead, he thinks, "What can I do to foster the ability for me to be able to do that again?" He turns his mind, his thinking, into a cause so that he can create the effect he desires. Bravo.

Last week his physical therapist shared with deep sincerity, "It's not your trajectory that impresses people as much as it is the heart and hard work you put in each week. It motivates other patients." That meant a lot to Chris.

But Chris' trajectory is impressive. I am happy to report that the curve has taken a sharp turn upward. Everyone is amazed. His occupational therapist said, "You don't understand, I don't get to tell very many people that they will get most, if not all, of it back. It's a miracle. You are a miracle."

I am going to do my very best to describe the incredible progress Chris is making. It's like sitting in the backseat of a fast moving vehicle and trying to explain the details of the landscape. I'm afraid I won't do it justice. Things are moving so fast that I am bound to miss something important if I blink.

When I visited him a few weeks ago, I watched as Chris tried out a manual wheelchair for the first time. He took a spin through

the halls with Isaac riding side saddle. When I returned
a few weeks later, he was only using the manual wheelchair.
The electric wheelchair was gone for good. Just like that.
Now, with a therapist on standby assist, hand on gait belt,
Chris has walked through the halls with a walker. He has also
tried an elliptical machine with a harness around his waist.
His knees buckled, but he felt proud of maintaining the stride
for a minute at a time. And, as of last Thursday, he has attempted
stairs and proven to the therapists that he could manage
the hurdle with a lot of time and attention but minimal
assistance. A landmark. This means we don't have to move
out of our house, which includes several stairs and no bedroom
or handicap accessible bathroom on the main floor.

And if those weren't enough, during my most recent visit, we
experienced something extra special. On August 14, six months
to the day after his GBS diagnosis, we were given the clearance
to go out on the town. A date. Just us, no therapists. They tell
us everything is therapy, so I was trained on how to safely
transfer him in and out of our vehicle, and we were set free.
Into the wild. We chose a sushi restaurant in the Haymarket.

We took inventory after rolling over to our table. No forks.
Just chopsticks. We chuckled at ourselves, not having thought
about that particular detail before choosing sushi. I waved
it off and said, "We can just request silverware."

"Let me try first," Chris said. He picked up the sticks, wrapped
his fingers around them and thought through the corresponding
movements. Sooner than later, he was eating sushi rolls with
chopsticks. Like a ninja. It's easy to forget that only a month ago,
he was still in an electric wheelchair with minimal movement
and little control.

The outings we were able to experience together while I was in Lincoln were educational. We learned something from everything. Unloading Chris from the car into the wheelchair and finding accessible building entrances. Reversing roles as I left Chris at the front door of our destination to find parking rather than the other way around. Experiencing a restaurant from a wheelchair rather than his usual six foot, two inch vantage point. We discussed every detail with hyper sensitivity, including how people reacted and interacted with us. We examined our self-concept and how this experience challenged it. Chris had not left the hospital in six months, much less driven in the front seat of a vehicle. He said the uncontrolled and over stimulating environment of the real world was disorienting, and the speed of the vehicle dizzying.

Our outings led to truly rich and deep conversations between us. Our favorite thing. After having spent several months literally not being able to talk or spend time together in a location of our choosing, it was perfect. One word. Perspective. This journey has changed our perspective in more ways than I can say. And I have come to believe that perspective getting is true education. Okay, maybe it's easy to say, considering things are getting better, but we are grateful for what we have learned through this experience. We are thankful for one another. We have respect for the tenderness and miracle of life. No, it's not easy. It's been full of sadness and anger and frustration. But it has also included joy, amazement, and full hearts. It has enlightened our perspective. A deeply valuable thing.

Madonna is a place where you see intimately and personally so many amazing things, but it's also where you come to know that someone always has it worse than you. For instance, Chris told me about a family who had come into the gym the other day. The new patient was a young dad who'd clearly had a severe traumatic brain injury. His wife, who was chasing after their toddling two-year-old son, was probably about seven months pregnant. I wanted to throw up just hearing about their predicament.

Another example. We were in the gym last week when a different family walked through. Chris said to the boy in the wheelchair, "Hey, buddy! Looking great, man!" The patient's family perked up with the thrill of having someone engage their son in this enthusiastic and, frankly, normal way. This patient, in addition to being in an electric wheelchair, was not able to speak and had very limited motion. He lifted his wrist and Chris exclaimed, "Wow, you couldn't do that last week! Way to work!" The patient's family excitedly suggested, "Give Chris a thumbs up!" I saw the young man's eyebrow raise slightly and he gave a flicker of a thumbs up. I lost my breath. It was heartbreaking, and yet there was beauty in that moment. It's hard to describe. I can tell you that my throat tightened, my eyes blurred with tears, and I had so much pressure in my face that the only thing I could do was look down and squeeze my lids together. Tight.

Over the last several months, I have observed Chris' effort to engage everyone at Madonna. The other patients. The other patients' family members and friends. Aides, nurses, physicians. Anyone who knows Chris is probably not surprised by this. I am not. I know these interactions genuinely give Chris energy. But what I have seen happen over the last several weeks is Chris' intentional effort to reach out to the patients who are not able to communicate normally due to their varying circumstances. He doesn't let the fear of no response stop him. He knows each by name and he says hello and wishes them well. He honors them with recognition. A reflection of their humanity. Our humanity.

This is just one of the many reasons why I love that guy.

13

when

the shoe drops

romance is a matter of perspective

I see you

falling, we go

together but separate

the long way

Mother Mary, pray for us

teach us how to live

the stuff of dreams

reawakened

on the other side of life

the ultimate destination

home

August 30-31, 2019

Chris and I took a big step in his therapy. We stayed in Madonna's transitional apartment for a weekend before he graduated from the facility. The apartment was built for patients and their families to better understand independent living before discharge. It was a simple rectangle that included a bed, bathroom, pull-out couch, chair, and kitchenette. It was a place to be together without the division of time and walls. The children took turns staying overnight because it couldn't accommodate a family of six. Those who didn't spend the night with us slept at a hotel with my parents. But while the apartment moved us a step closer to reuniting as a family, we quickly learned why the experience was on doctor's orders.

The weekend was fraught with physical and psychological landmines. The results of how well we navigated these landmines would give us an idea of what to expect in the near future. We started off strong. Leaving his wheelchair behind, Chris joined us for a walk through the city park using only his walker for assistance. I held onto the gait belt wrapped tightly around his waist, wondering how I'd actually catch him if he fell. He traversed grass, gravel, and cracked concrete before he successfully made his way to a bench where he could sit and watch as I pushed swings and ran after children. It was the first time we had gone anywhere without the wheelchair. The fresh air and sounds of laughter were intoxicating. The feeling of normalcy made us conquerors. We felt liberated.

The buzz of our liberation subsided when we returned to the apartment, though. By design, there were no nurses or aides dropping by to administer pills, helping with bed repositioning, or assisting with bathroom activities. It was Chris' responsibility to remember which pills to take and when. It was Chris' responsibility to determine how to safely navigate the new room.

It was Chris who had to determine how to budget his energy amidst a new schedule. My challenge was to balance my expectations of Chris as a dad and husband against his current abilities. My own selfish desires wanted to ignore all the things Chris couldn't do and needed to do. I wanted to get back to what we were before. Experience partnership again. I wanted the children to be able to wrestle with their dad on the living room floor. I wanted to "play house" with my happy family.

Those thoughts disappeared as I watched Chris battle competing responsibilities as he fended off waves of exhaustion. He had to think through his every next move so as not to take the wrong medications or fall after losing his balance. Juggling these responsibilities, while finally feeling and acting like a dad and husband again, proved overwhelming. Chris was accustomed to constant questions, but these questions came from nurses who asked if he needed anything. The children's questions were more demanding. They asked for his attention. For food. For water. For help in the bathroom. For a book. For a movie. For a different movie. For discipline. For soothing. For love. He didn't have the ability to participate physically, so he tried using his voice to direct traffic and re-establish his dad level authority. But eventually, his voiced raised to the level of panic. He lost his temper and shut down for a nap, leaving me alone and disappointed in our dark rectangular apartment with four children. One of whom was crying, two hungry, and another desperate for her crib. The finish line was a mirage.

Then came the anger. I was angry that I had gotten ahead of myself. Angry I had jumped into how we could implement a joint approach to parenting. Angry I'd believed we could immediately function like a family as we used to. Angry that we weren't already creating new happy memories together. Chris had made such incredible progress in his recovery thus far that I figured this would be the easy part. But independent living, especially when you are expected to care for little ones too, is an elevated challenge. We had so much more road to travel before we could resume normalcy, and it would be filled with unexpected potholes and optical illusions. And I was tired. With anger out, sadness soon followed, which stung all the more. I tried to crawl back under my blanket of detachment, but it was too late. A familiar pit formed in my stomach.

August 20–September 29, 2019 | Caring Bridge journal

What do you do when you find yourself in the valley of the shadow of death? If you have been following along, you know what's next. You don't pitch a tent. You keep walking.

And that's what we did these last eight months. We walked through that dark place the best we could. And now, just as surprisingly as we found ourselves there, the way is widening and everything seems much brighter. We can see a vast and brilliant landscape on the horizon as our eyes adjust to the light. We examine our new surroundings cautiously, though. It all looks oddly familiar, yet it's not the same.

Immediately after Chris was swept to the ICU last February, his mom cradled me like a baby in the waiting room while innocent passersby tried to avert their eyes. Lost, I rambled, "I am not me without him."

Three months later, when Chris regained his voice, he told me, "I am not me without you." He used the exact same words without any knowledge of my waiting room processing months before.

It's amazing how lives grow together. Like plant roots entwining themselves, cohabitating and mingling, and at times getting into the others' way. When you transplant them, you have to pull the roots apart. You hear (feel) the ripping as you tug. Over the last several months of being apart, we have learned who we are without the other. It was not by choice. It was by necessity. During this time, we have learned things we never could have expected. New parts of ourselves were revealed. Parts that were probably always there but hidden from view, unexercised. The familiar traits, those that had become our sense of identity, were tested. Some have dissolved. Others remain, tried and true. For instance, it turns out Chris' positivity is legit. And thank God for that. It has served us well.

This experience broke our lives in half. We now have a *Before* and an *After*.

But, at this point in the journey, we are not only looking forward to what's next but are also taking inventory of what just happened. Some of it was very traumatic. And trauma doesn't just come and go, exactly. I am figuring out that there is an echo you live with. Memories flash when you least expect them. That said, as painful as our experience has been at times, I am fully cognizant that our lives have new depth dredged by the pain. It feels real. It feels meaningful.

While Chris' recovery has progressed at a truly impressive rate, the last four weeks especially have shown phenomenal gains. During this time, Chris swapped his wheelchair for a walker. Then his walker for a cane. The cane now leans against a wall in his room, and he uses only leg braces for assistance.

Additionally, in the last month, Chris transitioned from the Madonna Rehabilitation Hospitals in Lincoln, Nebraska, to Quality Living Incorporated (QLI) in Omaha. On his last day at Madonna, September 11, he met his own goal of walking unassisted out the front doors. It was bittersweet as he said goodbye to his many caregivers and new friends. Madonna had become home, a place where miracles had happened. Before he left, he was presented with his second Madonna Spirit Award recognizing his positive attitude and work ethic. The local Lincoln television media even featured his recovery in a news story that highlighted the regional expertise of Madonna.

QLI is an incredible place specializing in the transition back to life for people with neurological issues. Although categorized as skilled nursing, it was described to us as a "kickass" place. And kickass it is. With an entire campus, Chris not only found his corner seat at the QLI coffee shop but also rode a recumbent bike around the lake on his first day there. Now Chris walks to his "classes" each day, which include regular physical and occupational therapy as well as life skills therapy. For him, life skills therapy focuses on the mental and physical preparation for returning to his many life roles and pleasures, such as husband, father, business owner, community member, etc. I am not surprised that QLI has been voted "best place to work" in Omaha seven times. It just feels good there.

A short week after the move, we celebrated Chris' birthday. While forty-three isn't an age that gets a lot of attention usually, on this particular birthday we were extra grateful. I reflected on the fact that we might not have been celebrating at all.

On his birthday weekend, we arrived at QLI and found Chris at the coffee shop. Like days of old, he had planted himself in a corner spot, and his computer was open. He was chatting people up and welcomed us with a big smile like he owned the place. It felt about right. Staff served us coffee, and we headed to the playground outside. On that beautiful fall day, while standing and watching the kids play, Hannah, who had taken her place on my hip, reached for Chris. Flattered, he took her in his arms, and she laid her head on his shoulder. It was the first time he had held her while standing since she was eight months old. Her little fists grasped his shirt.

We had an amazing weekend. Events included a special night out with Ben and Sam to the Broadway musical Hamilton. My dream come true. The next day we went to the Omaha Zoo, where Chris walked up and down the paths much like the rest of us. I never would have guessed he would be able to do that again. Everyone's feet ached by the end of the day.

As the weekend drew to a close, Chris said, "I want to come home." He said it while thinking aloud. It was a realization, almost a surprise. You see, his rehabilitation has been a labor of love. His main focus and full-time job. He takes it seriously, because he is determined to come home his very best.

Walking to the car and getting ready to say our all too regular farewells, we looked around and asked with a hint of panic, "Where's Isaac?" I held my breath and frantically scanned the environment. We split up. Chris went in one direction, and I went the other. Soon enough, Chris came back outside with the all clear. Isaac came shuffling close behind, head down. We'd had an attempted stowaway. As everyone else walked out of Chris' room, Isaac had remained hiding behind the chair. He purposely hadn't responded when we called for him. When he was finally spotted, he cried and admitted he didn't want to go. "I want to stay here with Daddy," he'd quietly sobbed. A heartbreaker on so many levels.

The good news is that Daddy is coming home. Soon. We couldn't be happier. Yet we find ourselves introspective. The care team explained that the homecoming can be surprisingly difficult on families. It's all about the reestablishment of routine, shared responsibilities, and expectations. Just like a group of plants whose roots were torn apart, we seek a transplant back home that provides the best conditions for success. Good soil, appropriate spacing, and just enough water and sunlight for life to flourish. We know a transplant can allow for greater growth and beauty. This is our intention.

14

when

the shoe drops

romance is a matter of perspective

I see you

falling, we go

together but separate

the long way

Mother Mary, pray for us

teach us how to live

the stuff of dreams

reawakened

on the other side of life

the ultimate destination

home

September and October 2019

I was thrilled when Chris transferred to Quality Living Incorporated (QLI) in Omaha a few weeks after our transitional apartment experience. Chris had made incredible physical gains at Madonna, but in my estimation, it was time for him to move on for another reason. He was almost getting too comfortable there. He wandered the halls with his walker, looking for opportunities to visit with others and share words of encouragement. *Lookin' good, man! ...If you keep that up, pretty soon you'll be running outta here! ...Go Twins!* His energy was uplifting, but I could tell he was ready for his next challenge.

QLI had been on our radar since the case manager at Madonna suggested it as an intermediate step before going home. We'd received rave reviews of the facility but were sold after a visit from a QLI admissions representative. QLI was classified as a skilled nursing facility, but it wasn't a traditional nursing home. It was a post hospital rehabilitation center for patients recovering from neurological injuries. What set this facility apart was its focus on patients' personal and professional success as they worked to transition back into society. Our experience in Madonna's transitional apartment clearly indicated we needed more transition time, and QLI was like going to college after high school. It stepped up Chris' game. He had more independence, but there were more expectations too. Chris walked himself to therapy with only leg braces for support. He administered his own medications. He managed his own time. He participated in regular physical and occupational therapy sessions, but his therapists also worked to understand his roles and goals at home and in the office so they could integrate strategic opportunities into his "life skills" therapy to prepare him both physically and mentally for the inevitable transition back. The therapists incorporated my needs and desires

into the equation as well. I noticed a difference in Chris'
confidence and demeanor within the first few days.

Chris felt more human again at QLI, if only because he didn't
see patients and staff around him. Instead, everyone wore street
clothes. There were no scrubs or gowns. No facility issued logo
wear. The absence of this visual hierarchy created a rich atmosphere,
one that beamed with personality and allowed both patients
and therapists to feel like themselves. The hub of QLI was a coffee
shop. Everyone ended up there at some point in the day to grab
a beverage, meet with a therapist, watch television, or make
their way to the gym. This beacon of normalcy gave patients the
practical experience of navigating tables and chairs and fostering
relationships. Chris gathered there every day at five o'clock to
debrief, laugh, and share struggles with his partners in recovery.
They understood the challenges. They lifted each other up.

Meanwhile, I did my best in counseling to prepare for Chris'
homecoming. The therapists at QLI had confirmed that the
transition was often difficult on families, and our experience at
Madonna's transitional apartment gave us a bitter taste test and left
me with mounting angst as Chris' homecoming neared. I could,
ever so slightly, sense my heels digging into the ground. I admitted
to my counselor that I was afraid of the inevitable disassembling
of my intricate coping system upon his return. The children and
I needed normalcy surrounded with firm boundaries for healthy
living. Nutritious dinners. No screen time during the week. Lights
out by eight-thirty at night. My finger on the pulse of how everyone
was feeling. I was secretly terrified that Chris' homecoming would
knock us off balance. I didn't know if I would be strong enough
to hold up the house. I might have to deal with feelings of being
out of control. And if I was out of control, everyone was at risk,
because I was captain of the ship and would likely remain in this
role for the time being as Chris continued to recover at home.

"Absence makes the heart grow fonder because you don't have to deal with the perpetual compromise in relationship," my counselor said.

Her words rang true. While I had missed the man, I hadn't missed tripping over his big shoes left in the middle of the living room. I hadn't missed the energy spent negotiating everything from what to eat for dinner, where to put the dirty clothes, or the preferred volume of the music. There were no power struggles or miscommunications between adults. No arguments. I had come to appreciate my independence. I liked being the boss because it was simpler.

I shared another fear about our remerging lives. It was more personal. I told my counselor that this experience had changed me. When Chris got sick, I said, "I don't know who I am without him." And I meant it. But now I had a much better idea. To some degree, I had figured out who I was and, frankly, I liked the person I found. I stepped out of my smallness to become more assertive and direct. I became a better mom. I implemented better processes to make life run more smoothly, albeit with a lot of help from my family and friends. I found I was enriched when I let more people into my life. I had grown into someone different than before his illness, and I was afraid I would lose her when Chris came back.

I told Chris everything I'd discussed with my counselor. The thing I value most about our relationship is that we always talk it out. There are no secrets. When I admitted my "letting go" fears to Chris, he listened and understood. He knew me. But I could tell he was trying to reserve judgment. I'm sure it didn't feel good to know I was fearful of his homecoming. Chris listened intently as I shared my thoughts. I could see him processing the information, applying it to his own reality.

That's when it dawned on me. Chris had been living a life without me too since he'd moved to recovery in Nebraska. What had he learned? How had he changed? Taking my best swing, I said, "I bet you've broken through barriers without me around, too. You are able to sit and visit with people for as long as you want without me imposing my timeframes. You can find new opportunities for connection. You can be yourself. A positive, motivating force... without limits.

"When you aren't doing that, you can watch television for however long you want without me in the background giving you a critical eye," I said teasingly. "I bet it feels good to leave your shoes in the middle of the room without getting snapped at too, doesn't it?"

His smile said, "Don't you know it."

Throughout our fifteen years of marriage, Chris and I had done our best to join our lives entirely. Support one another in our endeavors. Lift each other up. Our mutually compatible pathologies had complemented one another, spurring and encouraging new growth. In many ways, we really did complete each other. But even in our best, most sincere efforts, we had stifled one another's finest traits in defense of our own. I love Chris' big relational self. But because I am less extroverted, I had set boundaries for what makes him so special. Chris loves and admires my precisionist tendencies. But because he gets exhausted with details before I do, he had set boundaries for them, making my efforts harder than they would have been otherwise. This discussion opened a door of possibility. We both agreed that we didn't want to resume business as usual upon his return home. We could find a better way.

But finding a better way would take work. We were still holding hands as we approached Chris' return home, but it took tremendous effort. We had to reach over the distance of time and perspective. Our together but separate reality had taken its toll. Chris was experiencing the conquering feeling of victory over his disease along with the excitement of freedom. He was on a high. A mountain peak. While he was working harder than ever at his therapy sessions, he had re-entered the land of the living. He was thrilled to be able to attend a community lecture at a local university and a concert in downtown Omaha. I was equally thrilled to see the person I love return to himself. But I was in an unexpected slump. A valley. As Chris would describe the exciting events of the day and the number of repetitions he was able to do on the therapeutic weight machines, I would grunt, "Uh-huh, good," as I wrestled Hannah in order to put a bite in her mouth and one of the boys screamed in the background for assistance.

Chris felt disconnected, unaware of what it was taking for me to keep it together. Maybe he was just helpless to know what else to do. He was back, but I was still missing my partner. This contrast of realities was only amplified when Chris would ask me to hang on while he'd give high fives and laugh with new friends. We were, and had been, living different lives for long enough. I was looking forward to Chris coming home to "us."

October 28, 2019

The night before I brought Chris home from Omaha reminded me of being very pregnant. I had been induced for all four of my pregnancies, and on the night before B-day, while I was thrilled about the new baby's arrival, I also knew I had to say goodbye to the life I had come to know. This "arrival" felt similar. It contained the same nervous excitement and the same ironic grief. The children and I had established our own routine, our own life. I had come to know them in a way that I couldn't have imagined possible. We were about to disrupt what we had built. It was a wonderful disruption, but it was disruptive nevertheless.

It was late for a school night. The boys should have been in bed already, but I found myself not ready to turn off the lights. Isaac complained about being hungry. I groaned, "Oh honey, it's late."

"Please, can I have sum-sing to eat? I am soooo hung-wee."

I thought about it. "Okay, just a minute."

The boys jumped on me like a litter of playful puppies when I returned with a whole bag of fried chicken. I ushered them into the bathroom and spread a towel on the floor. With the chicken in the center of our huddle, we had a picnic. Isaac sat on my lap. Ben and Sam flanked my sides. Isaac dubbed it a "chicken powdy."

I made a toast with my water bottle. "Eh hem. Tonight is a very special night." There was excitement in the air as the boys waited for me to say more. "Tonight is the last night it will be just us before Daddy comes home." Sam burst into an outright grin, covering his mouth with his hand and rocking back and forth. "This has been hard. Really, really hard. And I want you to know that I am so proud of you. Each of you has shown incredible courage during these tough times." They smiled and bumped drumsticks. "I also want you to know that I am really sorry." I noticed the nervous looks they gave one another out of the corner of their eyes. "I am sorry that I had to leave for such a long time when Daddy was so sick. I am sorry that I didn't call more to explain what was happening. I am sorry that I lost my temper from time to time. I wish I could have communicated better."

The children solemnly nodded their forgiveness. Still a little hurt, Ben threw in a comment, "Mom, you should have talked to us more."

"I know, baby," I said, lowering my head. "Parents make mistakes, too, guys."

Throughout our experience, people casually made the same comment. "At least your kids are young. Kids are resilient." You will never hear me make that statement. While I agree that children are resilient, my children felt the weight of this experience deeply. It rocked their worlds. That said, throughout Chris' illness and recovery process, each of them gave a brilliant sneak peek of the elders they are to become. I couldn't have been prouder of their strength in the face of adversity. Their love and joy, power and will.

I thought about the time Ben gathered me in his arms for a twenty-second hug when he could tell I was upset. He had heard that a hug doesn't take maximum effect until twenty seconds and wanted to make sure I felt the fullness of his love. Or the time at counseling when Isaac described step by step how he was planning to rescue his dad from the hole he had fallen into. Or when Sam embraced the paralyzed Chris over and over, even though the horrible smell of pneumonia-causing bacteria seeped from his tracheostomy site. The smell was raunchy enough to gag a trained professional, but Sam powered through because he could tell the hugs made Chris happy.

The children proved that they are emotionally intelligent, fixers and solvers, wild and unleashed, tender, clever, witty, curious, silly, sweet, and hilarious. Perfect beings. Their displays of wisdom and loyalty throughout this painful endeavor were the most beautiful things I had ever seen.

October 29, 2019 | morning

I felt unbridled on my way to Omaha. It was a gorgeous morning, barely a cloud in the sky. Nine months after Chris' diagnosis, with one of the most severe cases of Guillain-Barré Syndrome that many of his health providers had ever seen, he had shed all his assistive devices, including his respirator, electric wheelchair, manual wheelchair, walker, cane, and leg braces. But, as I thought of all the other patients we met along the way, I felt survivor's guilt. There were so many stories filled with trauma, mishap, and heartbreak. I understood that every patient's recovery process is as unique as their individual situation, but I couldn't help but feel sorry to have realized such amazing results when others were going home in wheelchairs, never to walk again, no family in sight.

Why us?

I was not asking this question in the usual way. I was asking why we had gotten so lucky. Why did we get to survive our situation embraced in the love and care of our family, friends, and community? Why did we get to look forward to the continuing process of healing? I considered the long list of privileges and advantages we'd had along the way. A loving family who dropped everything to support us, a community whose kind and generous response had been overwhelming. We were beginning this next phase of our journey with a revved engine because of their love. It could have been vastly different. Had we been dealt a different hand, we could have been scraping by to survive, desperately trying to keep a roof over our heads and feed our children as we tried to manage Chris' wheelchair bound life.

I'll never forget one patient at QLI who had experienced a severe traumatic brain injury. When I first met him, he was sitting in the dining room wearing big facial expressions, speaking loudly as drool hung off his bottom lip in a long string. He motioned for me to come toward him, so I did. When I got close enough, he lurched forward and grabbed the two strings hanging off my sweatshirt. Pulling my face toward his, it seemed as if he was trying to kiss me. I backpedaled until he lost his grip, and then I scuttled down the hall toward Chris' room, looking over my shoulder precariously.

When I told Chris what had happened, he gave me the man's name and explained that he had found a nice rapport with him. Chris always mirrored this man's loud "Hey!" when he entered the room and gave him high fives. He told me that people with traumatic brain injuries often lack a braking mechanism for self-control. They can't restrain their emotions and often make inappropriate comments to friends or strangers. He said the man has a lot more intellect than you would assume. One night at dinner, the therapists were playing trivia with the patients. They asked questions from the citizenship test given to immigrants to the United States. The man had gotten every single question correct. Another time, Chris said he could tell the man was feeling upset. When Chris asked what was wrong, the man replied in his garbled voice, "Fucking drunk driver in nineteen eighty-nine." Turns out, this man had been walking across the street, minding his own business, when he was hit by a drunk driver in 1989, thirty years earlier. He was still pondering the accident that led to his debilitated state.

Why us? How did we get so lucky?

It honestly wasn't fair.

October 29, 2019 | afternoon

As Chris said goodbye to his new friends at QLI, the man who had been hit by the drunk driver approached Chris to give him a high five. The man shared a heartfelt farewell, expressing his appreciation for Chris' friendship and saying he would be missed. Then the man grabbed Chris' shirt, pulled him in close for a hug, and whispered into his ear, "Slut." With tremendous, roaring laughter, he let go of Chris' shirt and clutched his cane. Chris stood there with a smirk on his face as he watched his friend cackle all the way out of the room.

With Chris' things loaded into the car, we left QLI for the last time. South Dakota bound. Like leaving the hospital with a new baby, I kept looking around, wondering if it was really all right for me to take him home. We oscillated between silence, excitable chatter, and then to a deep discussion about the meaning of life. With disbelief, we reflected on our experience, knowing that we were being transported, completely transformed, through a portal back to where we began.

Father Richard Rohr says struggle and incomprehensible mystery are the ways to transformation. Our experience had definitely been a struggle, and in many ways it remained an incomprehensible mystery. But we couldn't deny that it was also transformative. I hoped we'd never go back to being the same. I hoped we'd be open to a fuller sense of love. I hoped we'd never take our lives for granted again. I hoped we'd always recognize that we live in choice. And I hoped we'd transcend the *Before*, making something greater in the *After*.

I remembered a particular morning in the ICU when I was heavy with guilt for being able to move my body while Chris was paralyzed in a hospital bed. Seeing his eyes open, I'd whispered, "Good morning. How was your night?" I gently put his glasses on his face. He motioned to the letter board with his eyes. I dutifully wrote each letter as he made his selections with the laser pointer. When the message came together, I felt a sense of relief.

It read: *I woke up with such excitement for all we are going to do.*

I looked at him with astonishment that day. Now, I glanced over to the passenger seat. Outlined in a blur of prairie, Chris was looking straight ahead. Resting his head on the back of his seat, a calm resolve had settled onto his face. I felt a spark. The kindling of possibility began to smolder, and instead of stomping it out,

I fanned the flames. There was so much work ahead of us. Continued physical therapy, trauma processing, and identity sorting. But I knew one thing. I had such excitement for all the things we are going to do.

September 30-November 8, 2019 | CaringBridge journal

A baby is considered term once it reaches thirty seven weeks of gestation. So, for this momma of four, I can't help but chuckle when I count the number of weeks Chris was away from home. Thirty seven exactly. Chris is back, rebirthed, after being hospitalized from February 13 to October 30, 2019. Cigar, anyone?

I drove to Omaha with childlike excitement on October 29. My feeling of anticipation was the same as when a child makes the long awaited trip to grandma's house for Christmas or when a young adult returns to college after summer break. I felt free. My windshield framed the wide open sky, and I could see the great expanse of potential on the horizon. One more family meeting with therapists and many more farewells to residents, friends, and everyone in between. Then Chris and I were homeward bound.

We pulled our chairs up to the QLI conference table and heard the assessments from each member of Chris' care team. The assessments were not surprising, but the insights gained, especially ones coming from a comprehensive team, were invaluable. Chris expressed his genuine gratitude. He looked back upon his experience and said, "Avera saved my life. Madonna brought me back to life. QLI taught me how to live again. Thank you for your part in my recovery." It was so true that it was profound.

We packed the vehicle with Chris' few belongings and then did one more walk through. Another empty room. Another transition. But this time, home sweet home. Like a new parent leaving the hospital with her fresh human, I looked around and wondered if it was really all right for me to take him home. Everything about the last nine months had been so controlled that even just the thought of no rules felt criminal.

"Oh, I have just one more person I need to say goodbye to," Chris said as we walked toward the door. Like a sucker, I fell for it. Again. "Okay, no problem. I'll pull up the car," I said before waiting another twenty-five minutes and wondering if it would look strange if I rested my head on the steering wheel. A meager surge of spousal irritation mingled with sincere appreciation for Chris' big, relational self. Things felt normal. This was normal. Just like the rich and meaningful conversation we had the entire way back to South Dakota. I shook my head ever so slightly as I worked to suppress a smile. I was so grateful that I just had to laugh.

I told the children that we would be home on Halloween. Just in time for Chris to go trick-or-treating with them. I wanted to make sure they had this landmark information because when in uncertain times it is nice to be in the know. But we couldn't miss the opportunity to put some magic into it. We schemed to come home one day earlier than they had expected. We wanted to surprise the boys at school. And, I am proud to say, it worked.

On October 30, we arrived at Saint Joseph School at two-thirty in the afternoon. The principal fetched Ben and Sam out of their classrooms. Without a word, they were ushered into the foyer, looks of confusion on their faces. "Am I in trouble?" they thought. Then Chris stepped through the doorway of the principal's office, and the boys rushed to give him a long embrace. At the same moment the boys saw Chris for the first time, the principal got onto the loudspeaker and announced a living miracle. She asked all the students to meet her in the hallway of the school.

Surprises are interesting. When truly pulled off, those surprised are initially confused. They don't give an expected reaction. Instead, their response is understated. A quiet burst of internal emotion that takes time to make its way to the surface. From having gotten to know my kids in a more intimate way these last several months, I knew what it meant when they buried their faces into the folds of Chris' shirt. I recognized the incredible joy revealed in the flicker of their smiles. Within minutes, their emotions bubbled to the surface, and their less overt reactions burst forth. They ranged from proclamations of a miracle to solo dance moves snuck in when they thought no one was watching. "I am going to call this a miracle. No really, I am! It's a miracle," exclaimed Ben.

As the students at Saint Joe's shuffled into the hallway, we took our place in the center of the group. The children and teachers bestowed their all school blessing song upon us, and we soaked it in. Chris seized the opportunity to thank the children for their many prayers. He told them that he could feel their love in his heart and that it meant everything. He expressed his appreciation for their support of him, but he said it meant just as much that they supported his family who had struggled too. Then he referred to the valley of death scripture and pointed out that in difficult times you "walk" through the valley. You don't sit down. The children laughed at the silliness of doing anything else. Standing smack dab in the middle of those kids, I took a moment to really see them. I won't forget those wide eyes looking up at us.

Fast forward to a week later, Chris' homecoming has been quite wonderful. A bump here and there but, overall, wonderful.

He continues to strengthen his physical self by doing therapy every day, patiently nudging his calves, ankles, and feet to wake up. As for his overall demeanor, he seems to be a calmer, more seasoned version of himself. He jokingly says, "And you thought you couldn't turn me in for a better version."

Our kids have been thrilled with their dad's presence and involvement in their daily lives. It's been a joy to watch them absorb what he has to say and then engage in playful banter. They have also relished their long awaited wrestling time with Daddy in the living room. The boys definitely have the upper hand, but Chris reminds himself that everything is therapy.

Chris has looked forward to shaking hands with and saying "thank you" to so many in our community. And now, here he is. Truly loving every conversation. During these numerous visits, I have heard him repeat a few select thoughts. He starts with, "This is going to be a broken record for Molly but..." Then he explains two things that he held dear during his most difficult times.

First, when Dr. Phil Meyer gave him his diagnosis, he said, "Chris, you have something called Guillain-Barré Syndrome, but the good news is that ninety to ninety-five percent of people are able to get back to life."

Second, after Dr. Meyer walked out of the room, I turned to him, looked into his eyes, and said, "This is going to be the best thing that ever happened to us."

I'd completely forgotten that these were my chosen words, but I'm grateful it had been one of my better moments. Although we are still unpacking in nearly every single sense of the word, I have found myself sitting back and wondering whether the last nine months actually happened. Here we

are. Together. Everything feels about right. While the kids
and I are emotionally rugged, Chris has come home to
a whole and complete family. No major areas of devastation.

And now, I must share my deep, deep gratitude. You, our
community of family and friends, held us tight during this
time of trial. There is no way we could have done it alone.
And we didn't. You were always right there. Thank you,
thank you, thank you from the very bottom of our hearts.

I will conclude with this. I know we are all interested in hearing
more about Chris' thoughts on the journey. But, if I could
boil it down from listening to him thus far, I would say
the following themes are present (think, fortune cookie):

The things you tell yourself matter.
A belief in something bigger is key.
Purpose is paramount.
Hope is powerful.

February 8, 2020

As the one year anniversary of his Guillain-Barré Syndrome
diagnosis approached, Chris and I thought a lot about how
we would like to celebrate his recovery. We decided that since
we started the year with something unexpected, we would finish
it with something unexpected, too.

"Wow! Can you believe it? It's been nearly a year since Dad got
sick. In fact, next week is the one year anniversary of when Daddy
went to the hospital and was diagnosed with Guillain-Barré," I said
to the children. We were eating lunch in a Qdoba after deciding
to take a last minute trip to see friends in Rapid City. At least,
that's what we told the children.

"Really, a year?" I could tell they were trying to wrap their minds around this concept.

"Yes, isn't that crazy?" I slowed down and quieted my voice for effect. "Actually, that's a big deal. We should celebrate, don't you think?"

The children wholeheartedly agreed. They are always down for a party.

"Hmmm, I wonder what we should do." I drummed my fingers, squinting my face and looking into the sky. "Oh, wait! I have an idea." I grabbed my purse and pulled out six pieces of paper, each with a different letter written on it. I distributed one to every family member.

The children were intrigued. "What is this?" they squealed with delight.

"Within those letters, my friends, is a surprise. And you are going to love it. Spell it out!"

Chris and I let them decode the puzzle. They begged for hints, but we wouldn't budge because we were enjoying it entirely too much. Isaac and Hannah had a big disadvantage, given that they couldn't read, but Ben and Sam did a good job of making them feel included. When their backs were turned, I rearranged the first three letters. "D—I—S—hmmm," I said. "Where to put the N, E, and Y?"

"Disney!" Sam hollered. "We are going to Disney!" He stood up only to land dramatically on his knees. His arms and face reached to the sky. Then he fist pumped while howling, *Yesssssss!*

Isaac ran circles around the fountain drink dispenser. He sang, "We're going to Disney!" He threw in a ninja kick for greater effect.

Hannah could tell something wonderful was happening. She looked around, threw her head back, and belted out a big baby laugh. She was definitely willing to go along with whatever was happening. Just look at these fools. It must be good.

Ben looked at us with big eyes and a hopeful smile. "Is it true? Are we really going to Disney?"

"Yep, we are going to Disney," I said with satisfaction. I was trying to hold back the fact that I might have been even more excited than they were. We gathered everyone back into our booth, realizing that we were creating a minor spectacle at Qdoba.

"When?" they asked enthusiastically.

"Tomorrow!"

Chaos ensued again.

As our family skipped out of the restaurant, dodging piles of snow on our way to purchase flip-flops, Ben stepped into my path. Standing squarely in front of me, he put both hands on my cheeks and said, "Thank you... This is the best day of my life."

Our little family community had been pushed to its limit of patience. The trauma of last year was behind us. The boys raced toward our vehicle, nudging each other out of the way to protect their opportunity to be first to grab the iPad. The baby, previously draped over my shoulder, was galloping to catch up with her brothers. Her blond hair bounced off her shoulders with each clunky step. Chris walked close behind, keeping watch over all of them. The children spoke in unison once the car doors slammed shut. I reminded them to buckle their seat belts. They asked questions about Florida, airplanes, alligators, *Star Wars*, roller coasters, swimming pools...

Chris and I looked at each other and smiled. In this perfect moment, I felt a sense of conclusion. The story we had lived the last year had finished. We were ready to begin a new one. On the other side of us.

epilogue

Chris describes trauma as "a thousand moments of separation" and recovery as a "thousand moments of reconnection." He is so right.

Like being pulled behind a fast moving motorboat, we bounced off the wake of our Guillain-Barré Syndrome experience. Our natural life preserving method had been to harden our bodies so the slap didn't hurt so much. When we were finally released from our turbulent ride, the momentum of our experience caused us to skid wildly off the surface until we tumbled into a disheveled heap. We were bruised and dizzy, but we got up anyway.

And we danced. We danced between trauma and recovery, separation and reconnection. We faced the honest work of breaking down barriers and inviting new growth. Sometimes we were graceful. Sometimes we stepped on each other's feet. Sometimes we accidently bumped into a wound that we didn't even know existed. I cleared the blackboard in our kitchen and wrote the words "Room to Heal" in large lettering. It was a reminder that living happily ever after is a continual process.

The miracle of grace appears when and where we least expect it and writing this book was no exception. It provided an opportunity for healing. Chris listened to every word of its development, asking questions about our experience of his illness. It was a way to mend frayed ends. Reconnect. Broaden our perspective. It was a major part of our recovery as a family.

Our family continues to create a thousand moments of reconnection. In our second chance at life, we get to practice being tender with ourselves and each other. We get to support one another as we morph into our next best iterations. We get

to watch Hannah blossom into the powerhouse she is meant
to become, someone who is just looking for reasons to laugh.
We get to smile at the glimmer in Isaac's cherub face as innocent
but witty thoughts bubble out of him. We get to see Sam display
his aptitude for mastery until he can't take it anymore and his
wild urge for horseplay takes over. We get to experience Ben's
deep and gentle presence, funky dance moves, and insatiable
desire to read late into the night.

We get to write books together, travel the world together,
raise great children together. We get to be together.

giving back

Thirty percent of all book profits will be donated to...

Avera, for saving Chris' life;
www.avera.org/support/avera-health-foundation

Madonna, for bringing Chris back to life;
www.madonna.org/foundation

QLI, for teaching Chris to live again.
teamqli.com/donate

Our sincere gratitude for what they do every day.
It makes all the difference.

acknowledgements

I am thankful for my husband, Chris, who patiently listened to every draft of this book, over and over again. This project was therapeutic in every way but mostly because you were my partner in its development. I am thankful you were willing to see from my vantage point, even when it was hard. You are my hero.

I am thankful for our children Ben, Sam, Isaac, and Hannah for their encouragement as I wrote, wrote, and then wrote some more. You, my friends, are my inspiration.

I am thankful for my book coach, Carol Ann DeSimine. This book would not have come to fruition without her artful process. Intuition brought me to you, and intuition is never wrong.

I am thankful for my developmental editor, Jim Eber. You remind me that when we dig deeper, we find the heart.

I am thankful for our family, friends, and communities whose support throughout the journey made all the difference. This is a love story, because you made it so.

about the author

Molly Weisgram is a writer who lives in Fort Pierre, South Dakota, with her husband Chris Maxwell and their four children, Benjamin, Samuel, Isaac, and Hannah.

Molly earned her undergraduate degrees in English and Psychology (2002) and her master's degree in Communication Studies (2004) from the University of South Dakota. She studied with the Centers for Spiritual Living and graduated from its Spiritual Practitioner Program in 2017.

The Other Side of Us is her debut book. In addition to her children's laughter, Molly's favorite things include soul searching, nature, and happy hour. She believes that life is not about disease, it is about recovery.

Made in the USA
Coppell, TX
05 May 2021

55054229R00125